Contents

Contributors

Robert Adam *Robert Adam Architects*
Robert Adam was born in 1948 and has practiced in the city of Winchester since 1997. His projects in the UK and abroad include major private houses, extensions to historic buildings, master-plans for new villages, public and commercial buildings. His designs have been widely published and exhibited. He has written numerous historical, critical and theoretical papers, published a book on Classical design, and a children's book on architecture.

Pi de Bruijn *de Architekten Cie*
Following his professional education in Delft, Pi de Bruijn joined the Architect's Department in Southwark, London and later moved to the city of Amsterdam. He co-founded *de Architekten Cie*, a four-partner firm, in 1988. The Hague Parliament project led to a series of 'old-new' commissions including: The Concertgebouw Amsterdam, The University of Amsterdam, the city of Amersfoort, and more recently for major inner-city mixed-use developments in Rotterdam (the Beursplein project) and de Kalvertoren in Amsterdam. His first prize-winning entry in the Berlin Reichstag competition has led to an assignment for the design of a substantial development for parliamentary use next to the Reichstag building. He is a master planner for the South-east 'Arena' subcentre and for the ambitious South-axis area in Amsterdam. He currently teaches in Delft, developing ideas that embrace architecture and mobility.

Sherban Cantacuzino
Architect and architectural critic, Sherban Cantacuzino was Secretary of the Royal Fine Art Commission from 1979 to 1994 and before that Executive Editor of *The Architectural Review* (1973-79). He is the author of several books on architectural historical subjects and architectural conservation. In 1996 he received an Honorary Doctorate from The University of York.

Edward Cullinan CBE
Edward Cullinan Architects
Graduating from Cambridge University, followed by the Architectural Association, Edward Cullinan spent a year at the University of California (Berkeley) and won the George VI Memorial fellowship in 1958. In the same year he worked with Denys Lasdun and in 1959 established his own practice in London. From 1968-73 he taught at Cambridge University and has since kept strong links with education as both external examiner and visiting professor to colleges and universities in Britain, the USA and Canada. Amongst other professional activities he is a Fellow of the Royal Society of Arts; a Trustee of the Construction Industry Trust for Youth; a Trustee of Sir John Soane's Museum; Honorary Fellow of the RIAS; Commissioner to The Royal Fine Art Commission; and in 1996 received an Honorary Doctorate of Arts of the University of Lincolnshire & Humberside.

Spencer de Grey CBE
Foster and Partners
After graduating from Cambridge University, Spencer de Grey worked for the London Borough of Merton from 1969 until joining Foster Associates in 1973. In 1979 he set up the office in Hong Kong after the practice's success in the competition for the Shanghai Bank. In 1981 he returned to London and became Director in charge of the Third London Airport and worked on the new Radio Headquarters for the BBC and was responsible for the Sackler Galleries at the Royal Academy of Arts. He is one of three design partners in the practice alongside Sir Norman Foster. Since 1991 he has been in charge of a wide range of projects including the new headquarters for the Commerzbank in Frankfurt, the Lycée Albert Camus in Fréjus, the Law Faculty for the University of Cambridge, the Great Court for the British Museum and the new Botanical Gardens for Wales. He lectures widely and is a Trustee for the Royal Botanical Gardens in Kew.

Mansell Jagger
Canterbury City Council
Mansell Jagger read Archaeology and Anthropology at Selwyn College, Cambridge before studying Town Planning at Manchester University. In his career he has worked for three major historic cities – Exeter, Winchester and Canterbury, where he became Director of Planning in 1986. He is a committee member of the Historic Towns Forum and has recently helped to set up a Euroregion Historic Towns Association with colleagues in France and Belgium. He has lectured widely and in 1995 was

Scholar in Residence at the Centre for Historic Preservation, Roger Williams University, Bristol, Rhode Island. He is married with two sons and is a keen games player, including the ancient art of real tennis.

Jukka Jokilehto
Architect and Urban Planner. ICCROM
Dr Jukka Jokilehto is an architect and urban planner, and is currently Assistant to the Director General at the International Centre for the Study of the Preservation and Restoration of Cultural Property (ICCROM) in Rome. He has co-ordinated the architectural conservation course (ARCICCROM) for many years, and is a long-standing member of the ICOMOS International Training Committee. He represents ICCROM on the World Heritage Committee, and his book, *Management Guidelines for the World Cultural Heritage Sites* (co-authored with Sir Bernard Feilden), has been widely disseminated. During his 24 years at ICCROM he has given lectures and participated in professional meetings and seminars throughout the world.

John Lyall *John Lyall architects*
John Lyall is an architect and urban designer with a busy young practice in London. The work of the practice ranges from railway stations, museums and commercial buildings to the adaptation of historic buildings. Urban regeneration work has resulted in successful projects in the UK, mainland Europe and the USA. Projects in Leeds and Cardiff have attracted awards from the RIBA, the RICS, the Civic Trust and Ironbridge. John Lyall is also known for his collaborative work with artists and choreographers. He is currently the RIBA Vice President of Cultural Affairs.

Richard MacCormac CBE
MacCormac Jamieson Prichard
A Senior Partner, Richard MacCormac is involved in the design of all the projects in the practice. He has taught, lectured, and published numerous articles on urban design and architectural theory. He is Fellow of the Royal Society of Arts, served two terms as a member of the Royal Fine Art Commission, and is a Commissioner for English Heritage and a Royal Academician. He was President of the RIBA from 1991 to 1993 and was awarded the CBE in 1994. Most notable projects include the Cable and Wireless College Coventry; the Garden

Quadrangle, St John's College, Oxford; Burrell's Fields; Trinity College, Cambridge; and the Ruskin Library, Lancaster University. He is currently working on the Wellcome Wing for the Science Museum.

Dennis Sharp *Dennis Sharp Architects*
University of Nottingham
Professor Dennis Sharp trained at the Architectural Association School and studied architectural history as a Leverhulme Fellow in Architecture at Liverpool University. He was Architect and Technical Officer, CTNW, Manchester and Manchester University from 1963 to 1968; Architectural Association Lecturer and Editor, 1968 to 1982 and is currently Special Professor at the University of Nottingham. He has received many rewards for his work as an architect and critic including a Civic Trust Award, the *Medaille d'Argent* of the French *Academie d'Architecture* and a UIA Jean Tschumi Award. Author of many books, *Place to Place: Emerging Architects in Britain and Japan* will be published in 1998.

Les Sparks OBE
Birmingham City Council
Les Sparks has been Director of Planning since February 1991. Previous appointments include Director of Environmental services at Bath City Council (1980-91) and, before that, the post of Severn Gorge Projects Manager for Telford Development Corporation at Ironbridge. He has also worked in the private sector and for Lambeth and Nottingham City Councils. Current outside activities include Director of the Urban Villages Group and Visiting Professor at the University of Central England.

Sue Taylor
Sue Taylor is a Researcher and Editor who has compiled and edited several volumes for the Institute of Architectural Studies (IoAAS) at The University of York. She studied the history of architecture and design, and has a post graduate degree in architectural conservation. She has worked in museums and on several exhibitions including *Glasgow Girls: Women in Art and Design 1890-1920*, part of Glasgow European City of Culture celebrations in 1990. Currently she is a Technical Editor for NHS Estates, compiler of book reviews for the *Journal of Architectural Conservation* and is carrying out research with Dr Michael Stratton at the IoAAS on Industrial

Buildings for the Regeneration Through Heritage project.

Paul Velluet *English Heritage*

Since qualifying as a chartered architect in 1974, the greater part of Paul Velluet's work has related to building conservation and development within historic areas. He has worked for English Heritage since 1991 and is currently Head of the Central and West London Team and Regional Architect within the London and South East Region. In an independent capacity over the last twenty years he has undertaken a wide range of architectural, planning, conservation, design and photographic commissions, and has lectured on building conservation and planning law. He is inspecting and consultant architect to the parish Church of St Peter's, Petersfield and consultant architect to the parish Church of Holy Trinity, Eltham. He has served on the RIBA's Planning Advisory Group and is a Trustee of the Covent Garden Area Trust. He has served on several committees including the Council of the Ecclesiological Society for whom he has been Chairman since 1992. In 1982 he was awarded the degree of Master of Letters for his thesis on the life and work of the church architect Stephen Dykes Bower.

John Warren *Architect and Conservator*

John Warren graduated in architecture in 1956 from the University of Durham. Early work in Pakistan stimulated a particular interest in the historic buildings of the Middle East and an RIBA Fellowship allowed this interest to continue, followed over the succeeding years by many further visits both for work and study. In 1962 he founded the architectural and planning practice of APP, retiring in 1991. Projects have included conservation work in Iraq, Kuwait and the Gulf – interrupted by war – and in the United Kingdom at Strawberry Hill and West Dean College and a number of important churches. He was founding architect of the Weald and Downland Open Air Museum in Sussex. In new build his work includes civic buildings, community housing and industrial developments. He is author of technical and historical books and papers and is a Fellow of the Institute of Advanced Architectural Studies at the University of York.

John Wells-Thorpe OBE *Architect Chairman, South Downs Health NHS Trust*

John Wells-Thorpe has been in private practice for many years. As a student he was awarded the Owen Jones Scholarship and subsequently the Andrew Prentice Bursary for study in Italy and Spain respectively. He was a Vice President and Honorary Librarian of the Royal Institute of British Architects, and later President of the Commonwealth Association. Until recently he was the Chairman of a National Health Trust and introduced innovative methods of design and procurement for capital programmes, which have been widely copied throughout the NHS. He is currently chairing a three-year nationally-funded research programme on Sensory Perception in Architectural Design.

John Worthington *DEGW International*

A founding partner of DEGW in 1973, John Worthington has advised both private and public corporations on workplace planning, design and management. He studied at the Architectural Association and subsequently on a Harkness Fellowship at the University of Pennsylvania and the University of California at Berkeley. He was Director of the Institute of Advanced Architectural Studies and Professor of Architecture at The University York from 1992-1997 and is currently Visiting Professor at the University of Sheffield and Deputy Chairman of DEGW International. He frequently lectures in Europe and Asia Pacific and is joint author of a number of publications including *Industrial Rehabilitation*, Architectural Press, 1977 and *Reinventing the Workplace*, Architectural Press, 1997. He is Deputy Chairman of the BITC initiative Regeneration Through Heritage, a Trustee and past President of the Urban Design Group, is a leading authority on the changing needs of modern industry, and has advised on the reuse of industrial buildings and inner-city urban regeneration both in the UK and Continental Europe.

Acknowledgements

The Institute of Advanced Architectural Studies has served the building professions for some fifty years in a uniquely creative role. By extending architectural education into the years of practice the Institute pioneered the concept of Continuing Professional Development in architecture. Through imaginative leadership its activities have widened the spectrum through building conservation, landscape and urban studies to project management and disaster recovery with a far wider periphery of short courses. Absorbed into the University of York in 1962 the Institute has broadened the vision and knowledge of several generations of professionals and university teachers. Since incorporation into the Department of Archaeology in 1997, the work continues.

This book is the consolidated product of a conference at the Institute in October 1996 and it is therefore to the Institute itself that fundamental acknowledgement must be made, and specifically to Professor John Worthington who took up with characteristic enthusiasm my proposal for a conference and publication to probe and discuss the contemporary problems of constructing **new buildings in historic places**. The occasion also saw, happily, the presentation to Sir Bernard Feilden of a series of studies in his honour under the title *Concerning Buildings*. Terri Tooms and her colleagues at the Institute rightly earned the gratitude of all involved for their skillful organization of the conference.

In publication the editors' prime appreciation goes to Neil Warnock-Smith of the Architectural Press (Butterworth-Heinemann) for his purposeful acceptance of their proposals.

The burden of executive editorship has fallen upon Sue Taylor, to whom both her editorial colleagues owe a profound debt of thanks for her unremitting persistence, care and tact.

Without the contributions – published and unpublished – of those who participated, the conference could not have led to this book. To them and those who have provided the images used with their contributions goes, with the grateful thanks of the editors, acknowledgement of the thought, effort and skill that has gone into their work.

Grateful thanks are also due to Gavin Ward of 'gavin ward design associates' who has designed the volume and made it ready for press.

John Warren
Honorary Fellow,
The University of York,
Department of Archaeology
incorporating the Institute of Advanced Architectural Studies

'.... A new building is not always to be dreaded, nor is a city or street necessarily the worse for receiving it. We do no good to the cause of conservation by springing to everything's defence. In this particular battle selectivity is all. The battlefield is boundless and crowded. We have in this country hundreds of towns of all sizes in need of new buildings which .... inevitably mean the loss of old ones. To insert the new into the old requires the highest degree of skill and imagination in every case. (Let nobody subscribe to the view that care has only got to be taken in 'historic' towns and that those less fortunate are not worth worrying about.) Clearly the deep-freeze glass-case solution is unrealistic and cowardly .... The rules are simple, for there are none. Every case is unique, every situation different. Precedent is an unreliable guide, judgement more important than justice, quality than period. Respect for architectural neighbours means more than the meaningless pleasantry. There are occasions for the quick return, the wise-crack, the spirited exchange between individuals ....'

Sir Hugh Casson, 'Old sites and new buildings: the architect's point of view' in *The Future of the Past* (edited by Jane Fawcett), Thames and Hudson, 1976.

Introduction:
managing and moderating change

John Worthington DEGW International

Change and contrast

The proposition that somehow new buildings with new styles are alien to historic settings is perhaps over-reactive, but it is an attitude that is frequently propounded. However, there is a long tradition of new styles being juxtaposed with previous styles that we have grown to love and revere. The great cathedrals were a cacophony of styles as they developed over the centuries, as each master builder added another phase to their distinctive characters. Similarly, the Oxford and Cambridge Colleges evolved and accrued, and Sir Christopher Wren had no concern when inserting his Classical buildings alongside the medieval Gothic of earlier centuries. Our acceptance focuses on the harshness of the contrast, the degree of sensitivity of application, and the speed with which the change occurs.

The pace of change

Over the past two thousand years of history, we have seen an accelerating rate of change. The first seventeen hundred and fifty years were those of an agricultural economy; the resources were nature, the assets land, and the institutions were towns. The second wave, which lasted approximately two hundred years, was an industrial economy. The resources were products, the assets machines, and the institutions were companies. In the early 1930s, the industrial economy was being superseded by the office revolution, the service economy. Resources were services, the assets infrastructure, and the institutions were bureaucracies.

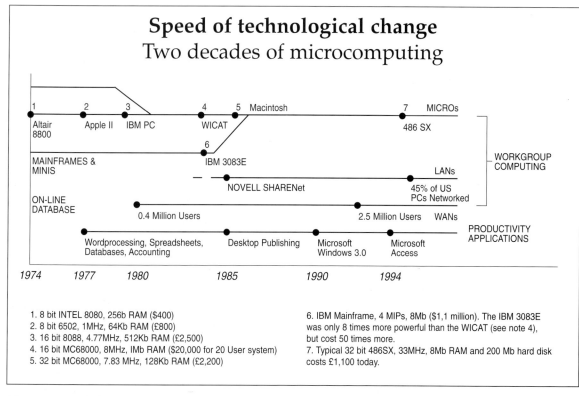

Figure 1: Two decades of microcomputing.

The service economy has survived for perhaps no more than seventy years before being taken over by the 'knowledge' economy spurred on by computerization. The resources are now knowledge, the assets networks, and the institutions are communities of interest. Perhaps this phase will last no more than thirty to forty years before being overtaken by the next wave of biotechnology. Within the last forty years the accelerating speed of change is exemplified by developments in computing (*Figure 1*). The pre-1970s mainframe, which needed whole floors to be accommodated, gave way to the 'mini' (1970-80), which was superseded by the desk-top personal computer with the mass-produced IBM PC of 1980. Ten years later the same power is encapsulated in the lap top and palm top, which are ubiquitous in every facet of life. Thirty years of computing have seen a dramatic increase in power, a shrinking in size, mobility and, above all, democratization of use. Understandably, planning and managing change needs to be at the heart of today's world.

To cope with this ever increasing speed of change there is a growing desire for stability, often exemplified in the concern for the environment around us. The more the social structures and technologies change, the greater the desire to retain and treasure the objects and places that we have grown up with, are familiar with, and feel emotion for. The popularity of the television programme, *The Antiques Road Show* reflects the broad-based interest and emotion for the past. Much of today's nostalgia for the past can perhaps be explained by a need to establish roots and markers in a rapidly changing world.

Past and future

The Prince of Wales's crusade for an architecture more reflective of the past, closer to those that use it, and building a continuity with past construction methods and materials, has touched a popular mood. At heart, his philosophy is founded on the premise of 'what I like is what I know', with the resultant falling back to the remembered environments of his childhood. It has been shown that remembering and celebrating their roots is the foundation of successful businesses, providing this is coupled with a willingness to learn and change for the future.[1] Sinclair and Amstrad were unable to move forward from their personal and cooperational management style, whilst Microsoft and Virgin, utilizing the myths and images of their founders, have changed to encompass professional management structures. Living with our historic environments will require the same sensitivity to roots, with a willingness to adapt to changing circumstances ahead. The role of conservation might be defined as the skill of managing and moderating change. The aim is to retain valued components of the past, whilst being prepared to take away pieces and insert new elements to meet the needs of changing patterns of activity, new life improving technologies, and allow the buildings to live.

Conservation, in its role as manager and moderator of change, is confronted with a spectrum of options ranging from doing nothing to new development (*Figure 2*). For archaeological remains, for example a Norman keep, the most appropriate solution may be to do nothing except record and consolidate the fabric. At the other end of the spectrum, as so dramatically shown by Carlo Scarpa at the Castelvecchio, Verona, by removing a part of the extant fabric and inserting a modern addition, new opportunities appeared that help to explain the original intention of the layout of the building.[2] The spectrum of options is broad, covering conservation, renovation, refurbishment, adaptation, and finally new build. The architect, by nature as a creator, whilst being sensitive to the past will be drawn to refurbishment, adaptation and new insertions. The craftsman or surveyor is concerned to mend and reproduce. The artist and architect by definition focuses on creation. Louis Kahn defined architecture as, 'the meaningful making of spaces in their light', a role exemplified by Pi de Bruijn's Parliamentary buildings in the Hague (*see section 3*), which weave the new with the old to make a statement about a modern democratic government that surpasses the mere reuse of the existing fabric.

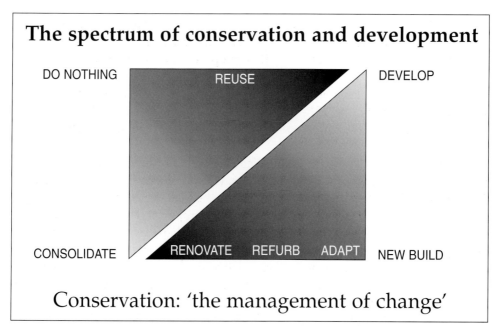

Figure 2: The spectrum of conservation and development.

Making choices

The rebuilding of Windsor Castle after the fire of November 1992, which gutted St George's Hall, the Grand Reception Room, and ancillary spaces, produced the dilemma of whether to reconstruct or rebuild in a different idiom. The press and professionals varied in their proposals from what was termed the Modernist or 'vitalist' to the romantic or 'ruinist' approach, with the idea of leaving part of the castle unrestored. Others argued for a 'replicationist' approach of precise and total replacement. Public debate spawned the parallel 'competitions' initiated by *Country Life* and Mark Girouard the architectural historian. 'A chaotically and dynamically inventive zoo of solutions and ideas emerged.'[3] The range of proposals was characterized by the popularist symbolism of Mark Fisher and Stuart Hopp's gold foil roof with a slit open to the sky, which ran the entire length of St George's Hall, precisely aligned with runway 09/27 at Heathrow. Richard MacCormac aimed to 'abstract the Gothic' with a structure that floated from the burnt-out shell. The traditionalist approach was represented by Roderick Gradidge and the decorator Christopher Boulder, who provided a reconstruction solution of decorative intensity in the manner of Viollet-le-Duc.

The final way forward was an option study taking the different requirements and approaches into account, and in parallel, the appointment of a design advisory sub-committee, under the chairmanship of the Prince of Wales, to recommend a designer. Six practices were approached for proposals to help in recommending a designer. The outcome was equally divided between the radical and the traditionalist. The Prince's sub-committee proposed the traditionalist practices of Sidell Gibson for the private chapel area and Christopher Smallwood for St George's Hall. The Duke of Edinburgh's restoration committee, after much criticism from Robin Nicholson, the RIBA representative, agreed on Sidell Gibson for both areas. The Modernist views had been aired and rejected for a traditionalist approach.

The story of the rebuilding of Windsor Castle encapsulates the dilemmas of inserting new buildings into historic settings. What is the meaning and symbolism? In what style should the building be? Who has the final say? In reading the story it is clear that the final choice of a traditionalist approach reflected the owners' wishes, but did it reflect the spirit of the time? Perhaps more time spent coolly setting out the requirements, and a wider selection process for design teams to be considered, would have yielded an alternative perspective. The list of designers selected for assessment was imaginative but hardly balanced without other respected additions with indisputable track records such as Sir Norman Foster (Sackler Galleries and the Reichstag), Sir Michael Hopkins (Glyndebourne), Edward Cullinan (Barnes Church), and Arup Associates (Snape Maltings).

Revitalizing the built heritage

In his perceptive book, *How Buildings Learn*[4] Stuart Brand argues that, through additions and changes, buildings and environments grow, change and mature. In his terms they learn and adapt to the social and technological changes around them. The King's Manor at the University of York (*Figures 3 & 4*) is a collage of history, which matured, changed, and developed through the centuries to Sir Bernard Feilden's final insertions in the early 1960s (*Figure 5*). Today, with the weight of the past, we seem nervous to continue the bricolage of development, yet, with an understanding and sensitivity of the past, new insertions in the spirit of the time could be the way of improving accessibility and utilization, and bringing new vitality to our heritage. Historic locations and buildings need to be used and to live. Like a pair of well-worn 'blue jeans' they improve through the patina of use. The good designer manages and moderates change, not merely to retain the past but to add to our understanding of it and to open up opportunities for the future.

The conference on new buildings in historic settings held in October 1996 at The University of York Institute of Advanced Architectural Studies, aimed to heal the separation between conservation and architecture, which has been accentuated by the Modern Movement. The chapters in this book, which emanate from the conference, argue from a variety of standpoints; but the overriding theme is one of appropriateness, and the need to develop and change without severing continuity

Figure 3: Entrance front of the King's Manor, York showing evidence of changes to the building from the fifteenth to the nineteenth century.

Figure 4: Adjacent to the entrance front, the 'Headmaster's House' by Walter Brierley, 1899. The architect confidently assembled elements taken from the historic building but cannot be accused of copying or pastiche.

with the past. Sections 1 and 2 set out the opinions of the philosophers and policy makers, who argue from different perspectives for continuity, and passionately believe that, whatever the style, good environments are the result of attentive clients and good designers. Section 3 provides insights of respected architects, through examples of their work in areas of historic importance. Each shows a concern for history, and a confidence about the vocabulary of twentieth-century architecture, where the new has been amplified. Today, the 'Modern Movement' is no longer a break with tradition; it has existed for over seventy-five years to become our tradition. I hope that the following chapters will begin to remove any barriers that exist between conservation and architecture, and to show that they are part of the same continuum of change.

References

1 LESSEM R, *The Roots of Excellence*, Fontana, 1985.
2 MURPHY R , *Carlo Scarpa and Castelveccio*, Butterworth Architecture, 1990.
3 NICOLSON A, *Restoration. The rebuilding of Windsor Castle*, Michael Joseph, 1997.
4 BRAND S, *How Buildings Learn*, New York, London, Viking, 1994.

Figure 5: The King's Manor, York. Sir Bernard Feilden's insertions of 1962.

Section 1

Setting the scene

Tensions exist between the purpose of preservation and the need for re-creation. The first, stimulated by the awareness of conservation, causes public alarm when residents see a beloved structure or site threatened by aggressive modernism. The second, directed by demands of progress and visions of the future, is relentless. Significantly, both sides of the debate are valid. A civilised environment should accommodate conservation and development in order to sustain continuity and rational discourse between architectural forms. The crux of the argument is how to prevent buildings from standing in opposition and producing a chaotic effect on the urban setting. The implication is clear, that conflicts between design ideologies are undermining, not enhancing, the quality of life in crowded human settlements.

In this section John Warren sets out the principles and philosophies that underpin our approach to new buildings in historic settings. He first seeks to establish who owns the past and lays out the concerns of the community, the interests of the owner and the responsibility of the designer. He points out that an individual no longer has control, but has to conform to a complex web of planning processes. Ultimately, the designer must have the perception and insight to create buildings that are appropriate to the welfare of both society and the historic environment.

The following two chapters present arguments for architecture from opposite poles of the spectrum. Dennis Sharp, from a strongly Modernist perspective, urges the contemporary architect to create new urbanistic opportunities for the future, whilst Robert Adam advocates a traditional approach towards creating something new, which may even invent a new tradition.

The historic context: principles and philosophies

1

John Warren *Architect and Conservator*

Summary

In setting the context of building in the historic environment, John Warren poses the question 'Who owns the past?' Over time the guardians of quality and well-being of our heritage have moved from the individual landowner to the community. As the author points out '...the Englishman's home is a castle whose defences have long fallen.' Within the architects' professional code of conduct the dual responsibilities to both the client (owner) and the community have been fundamental. With increasing commercial pressures, it is imperative for designers to be sensitive to the wider ownership of historic settings and to recognize the delicate balance that is required between personal innovation and the character of extant buildings and landscapes.

Warren argues that designing in an historic environment requires an 'awareness of historic circumstances and a sense of responsibility to historic evidence.' The designer with sensitivity to the historic environment is working within a fine balance. If the building is unduly historicist the environment may be forced to take on a greater historic appearance than is justified. If materials are inserted that are vigorously new and disruptive then the historic quality of the environment might be diminished.

From the historic context we derive scale, mass, texture, volumetric form and style. The historic is our remembrance and plays on our emotions. Style often reflects the familiar. If historicism is not to become pastiche, the quality of the style is dependent on the fundamentals of architectural good practice, integrity, texture, massing, composition and rhythm.

The concern of society for our past provides a valued set of checks and balances that should influence but not impinge upon architectural innovation and inspiration. The individual, whether owner or designer, no longer commands but has conform to a complex web of standards, codified wisdom and planning processes. The designer, within this complex web of accepted wisdom, must have the perception and insight to know when it is appropriate to change convention and, by so doing, add to long term meaning and value.

The question of 'ownership'

One crucial factor makes architecture in the historic context different from that same creative business elsewhere: it is that to build in the historic context is to intervene in an established social milieu.

The community, unlike the individual, has an indefinite life. Moreover, its concern with the built environment increases as time goes by. To eighteenth-century landowners and their surveyors the house they created was entirely a private concern. They designed it as they fancied and would pull it down as they chose. But they have gone. The house survives. The community now feels a sense of proprietorship and legislates to ensure that its claim is recognized. In this way the community may be said to invest itself in structures created through the work of earlier generations, sometimes to the point of exclusivity, when building owners are so hamstrung with legislation that they can do nothing to change the property, even if they want to.

In the historic context we may identify a polarity far more powerful and uniformly balanced than in work on the green-field site where the investor and the designer are the primary parties and the community has a tertiary role, reactive and limited in extent, creating as it were a field of operations uniformly applicable to all comers. In the historic context, however, the community moves into a pro-active architectural role, declaring its concern for all aspects of the historic structures: their grouping, uses and external appearance, their interiors, maintenance, funding – even accessibility. In historical terms the 'Englishman's home' is a castle whose defences have long fallen.

Concerns of the community

In the historic context the community has a level of concern that profoundly affects the nature of any intervention and may inhibit or prohibit change entirely. The underlying relationship, however, remains that of the property owner and the designer, who in rare instances may be one and the same. Outside the historic circumstance there is a two-way reactive relationship between them, complicated by considerations of use and funding and constrained by planning policies. With the introduction of a third party the triple polarity creates a six-way relationship as opposed to a two-way relationship. This produces a great increase in complexity with consequently higher likelihoods of mutually interfering pressures and reactions. The community enters into the funding relationship, aesthetic judgements and the problems of utilization. Community funding is added to owner funding and consequently the community expects to have a say in the application of those funds. It demands access. It controls materials. It enters intensively into planning debate, giving special weight to special interest groups. It draws its strength from statute law and national expertise. In this context the community takes on a surrogate (even perhaps a real) ownership position. Historic buildings, if they do not pass into its possession, become owned associatively by use and familiarity. The spaces between them enter into the public domain. Possession is all the time apparent – our town, our heritage, our duty as trustees for the future and so on. Overriding this surrogate ownership lies statute law, which defines – to the level of window and door surround – the historic and social interest of the community in the built environment.

Motivating this statutory concern is the informal pressure of groups, organizations and individuals – the voice of the people, heard sometimes so strongly, that a complete development may be abandoned. The very word 'carbuncle' has taken on a new significance since the Prince of Wales used it to signal his disapproval of a design. The acclaim that greeted his disapproval set aside the results of a fairly-won competition. His phrase 'on the face of a well-loved friend' emphasized specifically the sense of personal possession involved.

The community pulls; it may also push. It injects design proposals and provides funds for historic buildings and environmental works. It mobilizes support. It may also be supportive in finding uses for buildings and its role as a facilitator may decide whether or not a project proceeds.

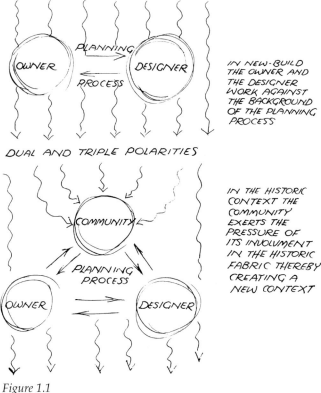

Figure 1.1

The owner's interest

A second pole in this balance of forces remains the building owner whose objective, as always, remains the investment of funds for a specific advantageous purpose. Even in normal circumstances the building owner may be coincident with the community and therefore represent entirely or partially its interests as in the case of a church, law-court or public baths. In the historic context this is increasingly likely to be the case, to the point where a private individual may sacrifice his personal interests in favour of the public at large. The simplest aspect of this problem is often the provision of public access to spaces that would otherwise be private with consequent changes in the pattern of use. It is clear that the owner's options are constrained by the historic context.

The designer's responsibility

The third polarity influencing the shape and use of buildings in the historic context is the designer whose behaviour is governed by an additional factor, an awareness of historic circumstance and a sense of responsibility to historic evidence. In some designers this is sufficiently undeveloped to be a serious impediment and a professionally responsible designer may, in such a circumstance, pass the burden to a colleague better endowed with historical knowledge or sensitivity. The term responsibility indicates an accentuated sense of duty to the community expressing itself perhaps as a sense of privilege and this in itself becomes a constraint on the designer. Beyond that designers are driven by responsibility to their clients, social duty at large and, that plague of all artists, the sense of their own artistry or artistic self importance. This may in itself lead to arrogance or the personal self interest of reputation making. These two incentives may themselves be in conflict with the interests of the community in the historic context.

Designers with sensitivity to the quality, or flavour, of the historic environment will find themselves exercising special care over the impact of their work. They will be conscious that the environment represents a statement in time and that their work can affect the apparent time in history that the environment displays. If the design is unduly historicist it may cause the environment to take on a greater historic appearance than is justified. If material is injected that is vigorously new and disruptive the historic quality of the environment will be diminished. Herein lies the important principle: that it lies within the power of the designer to amend by reduction or enhancement the historic context. The constraint is the designer's own sense of responsibility, respect for the established character of the environment and attitude to change.

THE DESIGNER HAS

THE OPPORTUNITY

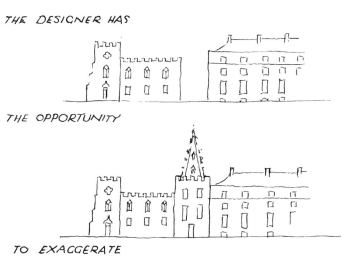

TO EXAGGERATE

OR DIMINISH THE HISTORICISM OF THE CONTEXT

Figure 1.2

The effect of time

The passing of time impacts on the historic context in two ways. Increasing possession of the historic space or structure by the community gives society a stake in the past. It may be argued that it was neither the landowner nor the surveyor who created the mansion but the workforce employed and the estate that produced the wealth to commission it. And the truth lies somewhere between. So when the heir passes the mansion to the nation there are those who feel that society at large takes back its stake. Less aggressively but more totally society owns the historic town. It uses it, governs it, controls it and defends it. And the two circumstances conjoin in the historic context to establish a claim based on time past. It may fairly be said that ownership moves continually in favour of the community.

In time present, the environment, as it has evolved, is the context in which the new intervention must find a place. How effectively it does so is determined by the interaction of the three polarities – community, owner and designer. But this is not the end. Their work is judged in time future when the intervention has itself become historic. In other words, a present judgement sees the present environment as it stands. The future judgement sees it with the intervention in place, established and accepted.

In some circumstances no alteration can be made but if an intervention is acceptable, it is by definition bound to make an impact. A decision made now is based on a view of the past. Its consequence is a future view of the present. Good citizens make judgements on the basis of their perceptions of alterations to much-loved places. But their children will grow up to look on those much-loved places committed to their altered forms. This thought may be rationalized: any intervention is judged in the present by the degree to which it amends the historic context and it will be judged in the future by the total quality of the amended result.

The pressure of buildings

One further factor enters these equations: the pressures of buildings themselves, and of the spaces between them.

We all know that buildings are inert. They have no active persona. We know this just as we know that continents are fixed and that mountains do not move. But continents drift and mountains heave: and we do recognize forces among buildings. We see them as mutually responsive. We talk of a dialogue between the railway station in Florence and Alberti's great façade of *Santa Maria Novella*. The effect of such internal architectural forces can be seen in the evolution of historic places. The erection of a column terminating Whitehall caused the spaces around it to be expanded giving us the present day Trafalgar Square. The power of the great western façade of St Mark's in Venice was such that over the centuries it caused the space fronting it to be successively enlarged to become what is often regarded as one of the most successful of urban spaces. These forces are not always those of repulsion. Sometimes they cause coherence and cohesion. Sometimes they heal wounds. The void left by a destroyed building may demand its replacement even where it is neither economic nor necessary. One of a missing pair of pavilions predetermines the shape of the replacement of its pair. It is also possible to conceive of buildings deriving mutual support: an inferior building gaining by the qualities of its neighbours.

Although these forces are conceptual, a product of the collective mind in the community, they are nevertheless real in the sense of existing outside the mind of any one individual. They are one with the social entity.

BUILDINGS EXERT PRESSURE ....

Figure 1.3

The multiple polarities of the historic context produce a complex pattern of pressures – the community interest, user requirements, construction costs, returns, subsidies, access, accessibility and so on. In so wide an interlocking of concerns and with interacting levels of argument at the conscious and subjective levels, the pattern of reasoning can be exceedingly complex. This type of complexity involving the community interest and individual interest is by no means unusual in human relationships. The law is full of it. Its resolution, often violently argued, lies in the balance of pressures acceptable to society. In the historic context society cannot afford to create such pressures as to frustrate the use of the historic environment, nor can it tolerate its destruction. Between the two it must provide a ground in which the new and old can flourish to the benefit of the owner and the community at large.

The designer and the administrator may find themselves in need of formulae and philosophies with which to describe or circumscribe their activities. These may take the form of rules and requirements, which must always be applied with the spirit and purpose underlying the combined objectives of historical responsibility and community benefit.

The interaction of thought processes may be expressed philosophically or as rules to provide a method of rationalizing thinking but, just as grammar will not produce great literature on its own, philosophy is simply a foundation for the logical thought processes through which imagination must move to achieve its objectives. The aim is an order in the assembly of ideas that facilitates logical conclusion. These rationalizations may be summarized as follows:

- In the historic context the community has a fundamental level of concern in the nature of any intervention and may inhibit change or prohibit it entirely

- The owner's options are constrained by the historic context

- It lies within the power of the designer to amend historic quality

- Any intervention is judged in the present, by the degree to which it amends the existing historic context, and it will be judged in the future by the total quality of the amended environment

- Buildings themselves exert environmental pressures by their very existence

- There is an order in the assembly of ideas by which the process of decision-making may be expressed in the historic environment

Historicism

From the historic context itself we derive scale, mass, texture, volumetric form and style. This last penetrates deep into the psyche and lies at the heart of aesthetics. Style is a language of visual terms, grasping at and being particular to an historical period. Style makes statements about history and circumstance, about erudition and social status, about origins and attitudes. It is a touchstone reaching the emotions, particularly of those who are historically well versed and probably, therefore, articulate if not influential. Style is a tool with which those who are skilled can manipulate the emotions of the viewer and since the historical environment is redolent with style new work can gain compatibility by its superficial application. Otherwise doubtful proposals pass scrutiny by virtue of phoney clock turrets and whole blocks of offices gain the blessing of planning committees and the public by having an overcoat of simulated eighteenth-century brickwork and fenestration. Much as they may be found intellectually wanting, these stylistic devices are pleasurable and socially acceptable. They touch the emotions and style in itself leads them to be harmonious in texture, material, form and scale. Consequently they appeal, but the essence of historicism is the creation of historical values and where these are fabricated they are phoney. This phenomenon may be entirely acceptable in stage sets, at the seaside,

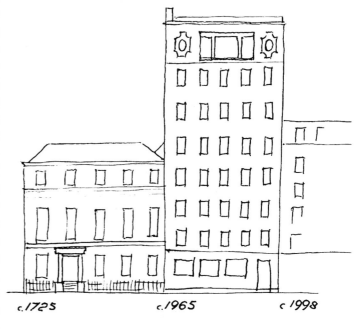

DRESSED UP 'IN STYLE'
ST. JAMES SQUARE, LONDON

Figure 1.4

in the funfair or on the pier and in the theme park. Whether it is acceptable in a genuine historic context and the degree to which it modifies the historic statement of that context becomes a matter for this debate. Historicism – the stylistic intervention – may like every other intervention be full of or lacking in other qualities such as inventiveness, accuracy, efficiency and it may vary in mood. It may be sombre, it may be gay, it may be wayward, capricious or exuberant. It may do its job well or it may fail. These levels of failure of success flow from the calibre of the designer but there is one special characteristic that goes with historicism and is peculiar to it. That is an emotive impact. There is in all creatures a response to certain signals associated with the past. The smell of woodsmoke, hay fields or incense, the sounds of voices from long ago, the travel down the road once familiar, the sight of a long-forgotten face, the recall of childhood places: these things all arouse emotions derived from experience echoing in the caverns of the mind. So it is that historicism plays powerfully on the emotions, lifting the half remembered past into the focus of the present. Like any powerful tool it has its place and an ethic in its use.

As a broad generalization, in the historic context the will of society tends towards a pale historicism. The stylistic dress provides an amelioration, a softening of impact. If ultimate acceptability is the criterion, there is no evidence that historicist architecture goes out of favour. Gothic Revival buildings are protected quite as fervently as the railway termini arches that were their contemporaries: St Pancras Chambers and Station in London where structures of both types stand side by side and are equally venerated.

If historicism is looked at as an historical phenomenon in itself we have a plethora of examples proving that it is a recurrent need, sometimes acquiring respectability in its own right. In the eighteenth century Horace Walpole pursued an emerging eclecticism with the aid (initially) of his 'Committee of Taste' and so gave a major incentive to the rediscovery of the use of Gothic styles, which, illustrating another truism, showed a pattern of increasingly academic correctness until the movement became dull and was overtaken. In a greater sense the entire history of Renaissance architecture is part of the same phenomenon, proving that a reassertion of style can lead to a new era of architectural innovation.

So historicism, however much it may be categorized as dishonest and therefore architecturally unethical, may be both practical and popular. It succeeds socially against all design theory and may also succeed in historical retrospect. Having forced its way to the table it takes its share of the feast.

Amelioration

There is another factor, amelioration, the growing acceptability of a design when once established on the ground. This softening of attitudes derives from two factors, the first being the diminishing effect of shock and reaction, coupled with the growth of affection for what exists – the 'getting used to it' factor. The other is the simple evolution of generations. To grow up with something or to mature in its presence is likely to produce love, for even a noxious environment. Thus it is that shocking contrast can become less shocking.

The incentive of winning popular approval can cause interventions to be dressed up in historical clothes, which to the theoretician is a deceit. A false statement about the time of construction falsifies the historic context. That this is an entirely abstract intellectual concept is clearly illustrated by the many-times repeated discovery that an historic building is by no means all that it pretended. Reflect on the cosy Elizabethan brickwork that proved to be good reproduction, deceiving architectural historians and the public alike. Suddenly the impostor diminishes in stature and becomes less worthwhile: and this although the building remains the same. The entire change has been in the mind. But it displays a problem that profoundly affects any formula – integrity. Without integrity the qualities of scale, texture, colour, proportion and detail are of limited assistance. Clearly a building that is right in all these aspects is less harmful and more acceptable in the historic context. But lacking in integrity it makes a false statement. It wears bogus medals on parade, which may satisfy the crowd but confounds the purpose of the display.

So the construction of any formula for use in evaluation and guidance must be one that permits invention and creativity while restricting visual damage and intellectual falsehood. It must, in other words, in some form be a sieve constructed of presuppositions that, if set down on paper, might include:

- Use of architectural style appropriate to place and time

- Volume and massing consonant with the established forms

- Colour, scale and texture comparable with the historic environment

- Usage that does not disrupt the established context

A designer working on a proposal for an historic area might reasonably make an analysis of its qualities on a sieving basis before making the creative leap and setting down an initial design. The client and the community might then sieve the design using the same criteria and this leads immediately to the establishment of standards that are widely, if not universally, accepted.

The structure of decision-making

Human societies operate, very largely, by opposing arguments – proposal and counter-proposal. Urban design decisions lie in areas where sophisticated, that is to say highly-educated, judgements are entered in matters where each polarity – the community, the owner and the designer – might be pressing in divergent ways. Whenever, in planning, such forces meet there must be an equilibrium achieved intellectually. Social organization has moved beyond the dominance of naked power. The Prince no longer commands. He may exert power by opinion but he too is effectively a supplicant in the planning process. While the creative skill that conceives, gestates and gives form to an idea remains the product of the individual, the context into which it is placed is increasingly codified. This raises problems of standards and their uniformity.

So we have standards of importance in historic and environmental terms, standards of quality and compatibility in design and standards of parity in the making of judgements, all of which depend on an intricate web of preconditioning. A cultural background pervades every decision and all aspects are so interlinked that no question of ethics, aesthetics and design may be isolated. The scenario is as complex as almost any in the gamut of human behaviour. Those of our senses that respond to home, city and country run deep. Orderly decision-making based on perceptive judgement is therefore fundamental to the welfare of society and usage of the historic environment.

Note: Some threads of continuity may be traced between the thoughts expressed here and the concurrently published British Standards Institution *Guide to the Conservation of Historic Buildings,* to which the interested reader may wish to refer.

Modern architecture's place in the city: *divergent approaches to the historical core*

2

Dennis Sharp Dennis Sharp Architects, London
University of Nottingham

Summary

As we move towards the end of the twentieth century and look back on developments in architecture over the best part of a hundred years, the Modern Movement is frequently blamed for what are perceived as inappropriate developments and damaging insertions to the historic fabric of many towns and cities throughout Europe.

In this chapter, Dennis Sharp, an architect who was brought up with the tenets of the Modern Movement, refocuses on the early ideals of Modernism and reminds us how it developed after the First World War when new aesthetic and social values began to emerge that were far removed from anything that had gone before. But, as he points out, within the movement itself there was a dichotomy between the Functionalists with their mechanistic ideals and the Expressionists and their organic architecture. In Britain there was also the Garden City movement with its 'cabbage patch' theory approach. However, it was the Functionalists with powerful advocates such as Le Corbusier and his followers that wielded the most influence and won the right to design the modern city with the organic Expressionists largely being left in the shadows.

By the 1950s there was a wavering attitude towards Functionalism. Influential architectural journals in Italy were making pronouncements against new buildings in historic settings and The Architectural Review, *which had promoted the Functionalist ideals in the 1930s, was moving towards a more organic view of architecture with its 'Townscape' campaign.*

Despite the idealisms of the century, we are reminded that in 1995 the 'Disneyfied' Las Vegas was voted one of the ten most liveable cities in the USA and that perhaps the most important aspects to consider in architecture are the changing cultural attitudes of different periods of time. Today's aesthetic standards flow from theories of deconstruction, complexity and chaos as much as from precedent. The challenge for the contemporary architect is to forget the dichotomies of the past and to create new urbanistic opportunities for the future.

Introduction

The Modern Movement in architecture was characterized by a dichotomy. It was divided over the way architects and planners viewed cities. The aims of modern architecture were seen as quite different from anything in the past. The traditional city had been transformed from a compact medieval place, centred on churches and dukedoms, to a table well laid out to display great collections of Classical artifacts whose ornamentation and expressions of culture were symbolic of new-found freedoms for church and state. In the Victorian period many of these cities were converted into 'Places of Mammon' and riddled with the eclectic demands of the new industrial barons of commerce.

Modern architecture had an entirely different programme (or programmes) for the city. It is sometimes forgotten that there was more than one way for Modernism to go. Indeed, at a crucial early moment in this century the Modernist camp was divided into two by the advocates of Classical order[1] on the one side, and those who supported the ideas of organic growth[2] on the other. A watershed was soon reached with the very different aims of the Garden City advocates in Britain, the Futurists in Italy and Russia, the Constructivists in the new Soviet Union and the individual Visionaries in the German Activist groups and the new Bauhaus.

This division may be described along traditional art historical lines. It is seen as a dichotomy between Romanticism and Classicism, between the Apollonian and the Dionysian and, more pertinently to modern twentieth-century architecture, as an issue between Expressionist (or organic) and Functionalist tendencies. Both had ways of dealing with cities, their growth and reorganization. The major challenge to Modernism and the city occurred around the time of the end of the First World War. This was a transitional phase. In a sense too it saw the end of nineteenth-century values. New aesthetic and social attitudes emerged. The *Zeitgeist* changed radically.

The city of contrasts

The early pioneers of Modernism, those architects, planners, artists and designers, who were interested in nature, in empathy and organic growth theories and ideas, predate the so-called Rational or Functional architects of the late 1920s. Functionalism itself, however, as an aesthetic concept (i.e. *Zweckkunst* or 'purposeful art') had been talked out by Hermann Muthesius and other members of the Deutsche Werkbund from the time of its foundation in 1907.[3]

The later so-called Functionalists promulgated the views of Le Corbusier and at the end of the decade saw the foundation of the key Modernist organization the *Congrès Internationaux d'Architecture Moderne* (CIAM) at Sarraz in 1928.[4] Technology (i.e. the mechanical ideology that had helped inspire the Functionalist movement) did not mix with the organic views of the Expressionists nor with the advocates of the new Garden City Movement, which began as a practical experiment at Letchworth in 1903 and soon spread out throughout the world in a wide diaspora. That movement, of landscape, planning and architecture, as important as it was, was rooted in a 'cabbage patch' theory. This was to find a suitably large area of fields in the countryside some distance from a dense, polluted and overcrowded city (e.g. London, Berlin, Paris or Chicago) and encourage a seasonal planting of conceptual ideas and you realize, *sans* history, the roots of an ideal city. Thus were formed many modern cities throughout the world, from Letchworth in England and Hellerau, near Dresden in Germany to the park and lake suburbs of Chicago.

The dichotomy thus brought to a head a number of important issues, some of which are worth reiterating today. They bring to the surface again the way in which ideas for urban design and the growth of the city, particularly cities with historic cores, might be dealt with. Expressionist experiments such as those at Magdeburg by Bruno Taut sought to renew the city through the introduction of colour, concrete, glass and new city 'symbols' or Crowns (*Stadtkrönen*)[5].

Figure 2.1: Bruno Taut's ideas for a Stadtkröne or 'City Crown' were based on powerful features that focussed attention on a city or region. Mont San Michel was one such example, which had undergone modernisation in the 1880s.
(The Builder *13 November 1886*)

New and old

In contrast, and it hardly needs to be underlined here, the popular conception of the Functional City was epitomized by such zonal schemes and proposals as Le Corbusier's *Plan Voisin*[6] (with its proposed destruction of most of historic Paris) *(Figure 2.2)*, the tenets of the CIAM *Charte d'Athenes* (The Athens Charter)[7] and the *Ville Radieuse*[8] project.

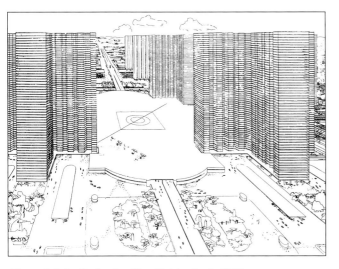

Figure 2.2: Le Corbusier, Plan Voisin, Paris 1925.

In London, the mechanistic transport grid city was further exemplified by Korn and Samuely's MARS Plan for London *(Figure 2.3)*. This was conceived as a total re-organization of London and a new transportation and social network (but with its historic city core left isolated but intact). In 1942, after the *Luftwaffe* had flattened much of London, it was promoted as a model for reconstruction by *The Architectural Review* who retitled it in their June issue of that year as 'A Master Plan for London'.[9]

Although stoutly defended by Arthur Korn (my own much loved and highly regarded Architectural Association teacher) as a *concept* needing individual interpretation and implementation, it was never to be read just as a blueprint; it proved to be a most influential source for British post-war architects and planners.

By adopting the zonal planning of the Athens Charter and adapting the clean canvas ideas of the Functionalists, the wholesale demolition and subsequent 'urban renewal' of large historical areas in cities took place throughout Britain, greater Europe and North America. The new was seen at enmity with the old.

The centre of Warsaw, recaptured in its original historical succinctness soon after the war, was an exception claiming that its reconstruction along traditional lines was as much for psychological reasons as architectural ones. Nevertheless, it was never seen as act of counter-Modernism but rather as a reconstruction that held a message for a nation. History was reinstated. Its architects and planners were, however, committed to the notions of the Functional City and the CIAM line as their subsequent work shows in their own struggle with the Communists who next wrecked the country.

Zero degree of architecture

The view taken some years ago by theorists such as the Italian architectural historian and critic Professor Bruno Zevi was that, within the Functionalist groups,

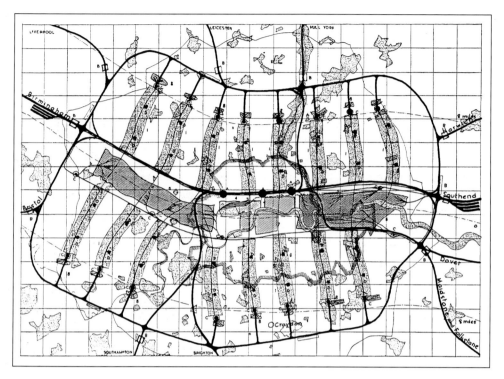

Figure 2.3: The MARS Plan for London was directed by the eminent German architect and planner Arther Korn, who was to be an influential teacher at the Architectural Association School in the 1950s, and the engineer Felix Samuely. The diagram for modern London resembled a herring skeleton but was divided up by wedges of green and separated into borough units.

a conspiracy grew up. It set out to marginalize any architecture that did not express the new aesthetic principles of the new architecture, which was characterized by flat wall surfaces, cubic forms and free plans.

At a recent event in Modena concerning 'Landscape and the Zero Degree in Architecture'[10] Zevi reaffirmed his view that the Modern Movement in architecture was never monolithic. It had, he believed, been a period of great emotional turmoil and passion that was close to nature during its pioneer phase but quickly succumbed to the dominance of the machine and Cubism in the 1920s.

Later, its apologists[11] deliberately left out of their historical assessments the work of those architects who subscribed to what we would now call an Expressionist or organic ways of designing. However, he concedes and deplores the fact that the mechanistic functionalists appear to have won the right to the design of the modern city.

At one time Zevi urged architects to seek a continuity with nature and with their surroundings. It was this point that came out again in his Modena paper when he condemned followers of fashion but saw enormous hope in the recent work of

Frank Gehry at Bilbao with his new Guggenheim Museum, Daniel Libeskind at the Victoria and Albert Museum in London and with his Jewish Museum in Berlin, all of which contribute to the cultural, economic and visual life of the modern city.

As further examples of the kind of architecture that shows a sympathy with the life of the modern city, he also cited the work of Peter Eisenman, Rem Koolhaas and, above all, the fundamentally significant buildings, landscapes and city interventions of the late Reima Pietilä. Pietilä, whose Dipoli Project (1967) at Otaniemi University in Finland began a new phase in organic architectural design, saw his own work culminate with the new residence for the Finnish President at Mäntyniemi (1993) just outside Helsinki. Zevi believes that the future lies with these architects.

The city core

Now let us look at a number of examples that provide evidence of the bipartite approach to city planning and the role of the modern architect in relationship to the historic core.

Figure 2.4: A successful integration of modern buildings in city settings can be seen in Alvo Aalto's work in the 1950s. The new building for the Institute of Finnish Engineers was inserted into an existing street in Helsinki (1954).

The 'Functional City' was conceived and developed as an idea by CIAM under the guiding influence of Le Corbusier. It derived in part from the urban experiments of Tony Garnier at Lyons and through the examples in his book *Une Cité Industrielle*[12]. But CIAM members came to terms with the problems of the city in a progressive manner dealing firstly with suburban problems and existence minimum housing at the first Congress in Frankfurt (1929), moving on to the hugely controversial session on the post-war reconstruction question of *Can Our Cities Survive?* (1942)[13] and building up to the historic urban core issues at Hoddesdon (1951) and published as a report entitled, *The Heart of the City*.[14] In it was stressed the importance of a city having only one core.

Eight years later, having left so many questions unanswered regarding the city and post-war reconstruction, this most powerful group of Modernists, and indeed the whole *Congrès*, accepted the fact that the *Zeitgeist* had changed yet again. CIAM soon died and along with it the strong ideological position of the Functionalists.

New attitudes were in the air from the international interventions of Team X[15] to the more prosaic side of English architectural journalism. How could a city have a core without a 'culture' was a central argument.

The Architectural Review, which had so vociferously promoted the Functionalist cause in the 1930s, turned in the 1950s to what it called a 'Townscape' programme. It lasted for over twenty years under different editors advocating a more pragmatic approach to city making. Townscape was a useful, if somewhat idealized, concept that had all the indecisive characteristics of English attitudes to design. It consisted of 'An infinity of particular ways out.'[16]

But what was this attitude really about? Was it concerned with modernization anymore? Or, was this a new way? 'Townscape', *The Architectural Review* claimed, 'is something bigger than individual buildings, modern architecture or the whole professional idea of architecture and planning'. Such arrogance no longer impresses but its aims do.[17]

'Townscape,' its editorial 'puffers' went on, 'is the visible expression of collective life, man coming together ...to make a higher organism.' Such statements were clearly meant to emphasize the role of the public significance of spaces and features in cities. It was not as totalitarian nor as Darwinian as it sounds. But it did lead to more words and sketches than physical results .

In the growing optimistic mood of post-war Britain in the 1960s the nature of public spaces owned by local authorities were quite different from private spaces owned by individual businesses as the Civic Trust – who built quickly on the *Review's* Townscape ideas – soon discovered. It began a community improvement exercise with its collective street rehabilitation schemes in places like Norwich, Windsor and Burslem.

Inserting the modern

But what about modern buildings inserted into existing urban environments? Here some real problems have emerged between those designers of one-off buildings who advocate a policy of contrast between old and new and with the use of new materials and those who support the conservationist 'Blenders and Melders'. It is this latter band who sought to integrate the new into the old and a reciprocity of styles and means of expression.

On this point it is worth recalling Zevi's words again. In an editorial in his magazine *L'Architettura* as long ago as September, 1956 he wrote that the construction of new buildings in historic areas in Italy 'has been disastrous'. He conceded that here was a paradox in the sense that it also 'implies an incompatibility between the ancient and the modern', which was not necessarily the case. Modern architecture, he claimed, should be able to to keep in touch with the past without destroying it and without renouncing its own means of expression.

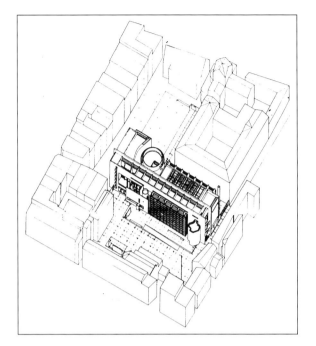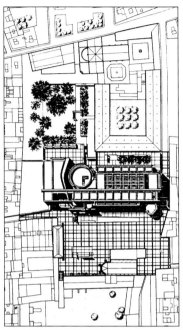

Figure 2.5: Museum of Contemporary Art, Barcelona (1987-92); Richard Meier's characteristic modern white architecture has invaded many cities and often offers a remarkable contrast to the existing urban fabric of cities such as Frankfurt am Main and Barcelona.

This was something that was demonstrated later in Venice by architects of the calibre of Carlo Scarpa.

One side of the dichotomous development of the Modern Movement that we have spoken of was the 'organic', a term applied to the natural growth of cities and a concept at the very core of the work of the American architect Frank Lloyd Wright. For Wright the 'natural' city was based on democratic principles and embodied in his design of Broadacre City (1932). Broadacre was to be a political place where history was to be made rather than preserved. Although controlled by plot size and an agrarian philosophy, it has over the years undoubtedly engendered an American desire for generous, expansive, decentralized and ever extending boundaries. This is seen in the new desert cities like Phoenix, Arizona and 'edge' cities like Los Angeles.

The ubiquitous Las Vegas is something else – one of the current typical examples of the 'Disneyfication' of American life that creates, often remarkably so, its own versions of history. One of its more recent escapades, the building of the Great Pyramid Hotel which, even when scaled correctly, remains somewhat unconvincing as a work of architecture with its black plastic finishes and Sphinx entrances. Nevertheless, it is by its very presence in shape and form a symbolical element in a city sated with such *kitsch*; and *kitsch* too has a history!

But perhaps we should let society be the judge in these matters. Compare the English. The partial reconstructions of country towns into historic pastiches are little better than the confections of Las Vegas. They offer an all too easy compromise that misses out the modern altogether in the conviction that the false umbrella of sentimental historicism is a respectable way to go. Try a market day in Totnes, Devon where decent people dress up to classify themselves as servants of the town environment. This device is just as false and devious as those who serve Virginian Shaker towns or *Parc Asterix* near Paris. It is basically commercial and culturally unsound.

Do we have lessons to learn here that cannot be found in a reappraisal of the Modern Movement's longing for social significance and aesthetic relevance? Let us not forget, harking back to Las Vegas for a moment, that in 1995 it was voted one of the ten most livable cities in the USA. It is of course modern but its modernity has little to do with Functionalist or Expressionist dreams of a world of new architectural possibilities. This concept was to be transformed by modern materials, light, colour, city points and cultural grace.

Equally it had less to do with Le Corbusier and the *Ville Radieuse* and perhaps even less with Frank Lloyd Wright's dream of the democratically decentralized city that could be built horizontally on a great tract of rural land. But even with his views, as powerfully stated as they were in drawings and rhetorical statements, his proposals for the rural Broadacre City were radically altered later in his career to accommodate that most American of all building types the skyscraper, a species that Wright himself called 'a natural American achievement'. Wright's own ideal city ideas were soon supplemented by the need to incorporate the high building. One even was built, the Price Tower in Oklahoma. Another, the 'Mile High' scheme was destined for the great Metropolitan centre of Chicago.

So Modernism does not have anything like a balanced face and Wright, for one, was supported in his productive and changing attitudes by thinkers as influential as Henry Russell Hitchcock and Lewis Mumford. Mumford's views are hardly quoted today in this age of instant opinions and computerized SIM Cities, but looking at some of the arguments he put forward, he can be seen as one of this century's most radical thinkers about the modern city.

He viewed the city generally through its various period histories, through its organic growth and sources, its functions

Figure 2.6: Tadao Ando's celebrated Times *building with the extension,* Times II, *1984, located in downtown Kyoto. It is a sensitive modern addition in an historic area of the city.*

and symbolic significance and means of expression. It was a centre of technological and socio-economic expressiveness based on the most fundamental spiritual and societal issues, i.e. fantasy and myths, on legends, monumentality, symbolism and style. Mumford claimed in his famous essay of 1951[18] that modern architecture crystallized at the moment when people realized that the older modes of symbolism no longer spoke to modern man; a moment when, on the contrary, the new functions brought in by the machine had something special to say to mankind. Thus, unfortunately, Mumford claimed, 'in the act of realizing these new truths mechanical functions have tended to absorb expression... As a result the architectural imagination has...become impoverished...' He claimed that the machine can no more adequately symbolize our culture than can a Greek temple or a Renaissance palace.

Conclusion

Much of this chapter has been devoted to the aims of Modernists and the city, its planning and organization. Perhaps more needs to be said about aesthetics and the changing attitudes and modes of different periods in time. Here there has been a more noticeable change. Nowhere of course is this more pronounced than in the cultural cores of cities when public life coalesces with private pursuits and where the fragmentary forms of individualism mix so readily with the bolder designs for public buildings. It can be observed in the ever-changing individualistic commercial shop fronts of, for example, London's New Bond Street, which are in sharp contrast with the more staid, but static, listed buildings serving public causes.

In such contexts the modern and the traditional co-exist, often for a temporary period, becoming inextricably mixed. One quickly discovers that 'new buildings in old settings' and 'old buildings in new settings' are very much part of the same discussion. Each reflects its own timely aesthetic.

As Gunter Behnisch has said, 'The old is not new', thus, the new can never be old. It is illogical therefore for it to even acknowledge the past, although it might take into account matters of scale and taste and height and also respect scale and volume. But if we turn to magnitude and mixed uses then, clearly, even at the level of the architect's brief, all things may well have changed, hence the essential intrusion of the large scale department store into the fabric of a country town or the skyscraper into a medievalizing business district.

Today's aesthetic standards flow from theories of deconstruction, complexity and chaos as much as from precedent. Architects should be able to deal with this as a conceptual change. It is so fundamental as to have already formed a language of new forms. We have already noted this in the work of architects from Piëtila to Gehry.

Figure 2.7: Michael Hopkins and Partners. The creation of a new road façade to Lord's Cricket Ground was the bonus in the rebuilding of the Mound Stand.

Figure 2.8: Santiago Calatrava. The insertion of an underground meeting room in the Piazza Espana, Alcoy, Spain (1991-95). The effectiveness of this intervention is that the building entrance rises out of the flat square, in order to gain access to the underground room, otherwise the Piazza remains intact.

What many fear is the undermining of homogeneity and orthodoxy when new and often unprecedented demands are placed on the existing fabric of a city. This can be created by the demands of a new research department or through the more contemporary acts of discarding huge complex structures like county halls (e.g. Westminster) or large-scale hospitals.

Are these causes now to be left to market forces and to designers' skills? These acts of change that we now term 'urban interventions' or acts of 'city regeneration', are being actively pursued, as well as in London, in places from Singapore to Bilbao and Oslo.[19] Through them a new urban richness can be created that is connective, flexible and dynamic. A new modern scenario can thus be built up to create dynamic 'core' areas for the cities and diversity introduced onto sites without violent upheaval to existing building fabrics.

Here at least we have one component of the modern city that combines the old with the new and challenges the contemporary architect to forget the dichotomies of the past and seek a creative future with new urbanistic challenges on a scale undreamed of by CIAM some seventy years ago.

Notes and references

1 For example, Camillo Sitte (1843–1903) a Viennese planner who was opposed to the planning of grand vistas and axes, sought a closer relationship between the irregularities of earlier city forms and the layout of spaces and squares.

2 Examples include Ebenezer Howard (1850–1928) and Patrick Geddes (1854–1932) who established a town-planning theory based on organic and civic values.

3 The Deutscher Werkbund (German Arts and Crafts Association) founded in 1907, aimed at 'the improvement of industrial products through the combined efforts of artists, industrialists and craftsmen.' After the 1914–18 war it became more concerned with housing.

4 The first meeting of the CIAM in 1928 was attended by some of Europe's leading planners and architects. It remained for over thirty years the medium of world-wide interchange of ideas, which brought 'urban planning' into perspective through its congresses.

5 Bruno Taut was municipal architect to Magdeburg, 1921–24.

6 The '*Plan Voisin*' was a provocative scheme for inserting huge concrete and glass skyscrapers in the centre of Paris, exhibited at the 1925 *Exposition des arts Décoratifs.*

7 The fourth meeting of CIAM in 1933 'The Functional City' addressed the problem of the modern city and town planning. The results of the deliberations were later set out by Le Corbusier in *La Charte d'Athènes*, published in 1943.

8 Le Corbusier's plan, c.1930, for a densely populated area that was given over to large zones of leisure including parks and playing fields etc.

9 'A Master Plan for London' based on the 1938 MARS Plan was published in *The Architectural Review*, June 1942. See also SHARP, D (ed.) *Planning and Architecture*, London 1967, pp.166–8.

10 *Paesaggistica e Linguaggio Grado Zero dell'Architettura,* Conference, Modena, September 1997.

11 Giedion's *Space, Time and Architecture*, Cambridge, Massachusetts, 1941 left out Aalto. Hitchcock lost faith in Wright.

12 Tony Garnier published his proposals in *Une Cité Industrielle*, Paris, 1917, although they were exhibited as early as 1904. Some of his ideas were realized in Lyons where he was City Architect.

13 SERT, J L, *Can Our Cities Survive?*, Cambridge, Massachusetts, and London 1942.

14 ROGERS, E N, SERT, J L, & TYRWHYTT, J (eds.) *The Heart of the City*, New York and London, 1952.

15 'Team X' was an international group of young architects who eventually replaced the older generation of architects of CIAM after CIAM X.

16 *The Architectural Review,* February 1964, p.91.

17 Compare with Richard Sennet's more recent study *The Role of Public Man*, London, 1978.

18 MUMFORD, Lewis, *Art and Technics,* New York, 1951, p.114. For the widest interpretations of the Modern in the context of the old see Mumford's monumental *The Culture of Cities*, New York, 1938, which discusses shifts from cathedral squares to the industrial 'non-city'.

19 See particularly the 'redemptive' work of eminent architects in Bilbao where Frank Gehry, Norman Foster, Santiago Calatrava and others have been brought in to transform this old industrial city into a 'modern' one. See SHARP, Dennis, (ed.) *Bilbao 2000: Architecture and Regeneration.* Book Art, 1995.

Tradition: the driving force of urban identity 3

Robert Adam *Robert Adam Architects*

Summary

Robert Adam is a modern architect who creates 'traditional' designs. In this chapter he attacks the Modernist approach to architecture, which he sees as self-indulgence on the part of the architect and alien to most ordinary people. He suggests that it creates a gulf between its creators and the public and is damaging to its surroundings.

Instead, he advocates an approach based on tradition, which he sees as intimately connected with the 'new'. He explains how traditions are created and points out that, although institutions such as parliament and the military are rigidly founded on traditions, which are still evident in the ceremonies they perform and the way they present themselves for such occasions, they are continually changing and modernizing to meet the requirements of the present day.

He sees architecture as part of our traditional culture and argues that instead of undermining it tradition should be used to create something new; traditional design can be original, creative and it can even invent new traditions.

Introduction

Two fallacies underlie conventional architectural and artistic thought, which have created a huge gulf between people and art this century. The first fallacy is that history is something external or optional. The second is that the use of history is something different from being modern. We are so used to these assumptions that they are rarely challenged.

New buildings and historic settings are, for example, set up as natural opposites and we use context or history as optional extras. Although these are new ideas, it is often claimed that they were in the mind of previous generations, but this is an anachronism. Architects of the past did not set out to cut themselves off from history; on the contrary, they usually tried to recreate an imagined history. While they looked to the past they were being modern.

There is no conflict between modern buildings and history. If you have a theory that compels you to prove in some abstract sense that you are 'of your time', then the use of history or new buildings in historic settings can be a problem. But it is not a natural problem, it is self-generated. It is a problem that has created a negative public reaction to new buildings. Architects design buildings they know are not liked, justified by ideals exclusive to architects or the arts community. The public has no interest in these theories or their product.

Figure 3.1: Chester, the honestly modern in an historic setting, a needless contradiction created by architects for architects.

Modernist architectural ideas, such as buildings being honest or bogus, ethical or unethical, are alien to ordinary people. The idea that to be a serious artist or architect will naturally involve work that will upset people and the idea that artistic self-expression is more important than the pleasure of the ordinary citizen are exclusive to the arts community. Accepted as universal truths by artists and architects, these principles cannot stand up to the most elementary test of truth – universality. If they are true, then most historic art was untruthful.

Tradition or custom?

The gulf created between the wider public and the arts community is damaging to the arts and to our surroundings. It would be much more satisfactory if we could share the easy way that ordinary people live with their history. This is not a history that can be taken up or put down, it is our culture. It is the thing that makes us European, British, English, from York, from our families. It is tradition.

Tradition is the foundation of our language, it is in our government, our family life and our food, it is in our cities and our buildings. When people demand buildings that 'fit in' they often ask for traditional buildings. Although architects usually think this is wrong, tradition is intimately connected with new things.

If we can understand how tradition works then we have the key to the easy relationship between new design and the history that saturates our cultural existence. The dictionary only takes us so far: a tradition is defined as a tale, belief or practice handed down from generation to generation. To understand it better we need the famous man from Mars who will come down from outer space and find out about traditions with only the physical evidence in front of him. And we do have our own Martians, we have archaeologists. When archaeologists look at pre-historic material they only have physical evidence. With this, they have to find out if something they have unearthed is part of a traditional way of doing things. Without written or oral evidence, however, they cannot tell if it is part of a custom or tradition.

What is a custom? A custom is an established way of doing something – something that is just done that way. In Britain we do not eat horse meat or frogs' legs, while in France they are eaten. While Britons in Britain are not offered horse meat or frogs' legs in butcher's shops and think no more of it, it is a custom. But, for a Briton living in France a deliberate choice not to eat horse meat or frogs' legs exactly because he or she is British would be to practice a tradition.

We can see why archaeologists need written or oral evidence to tell the difference. We can also see the relationship between custom and tradition. Tradition is deliberate and custom is not. Tradition can be consciously preserved custom and, above all, it must be conscious. But how does an archaeologist tell if something found was part of a custom or tradition? It is only possible to tell if there is evidence

Figure 3.2: Through the study of Prehistory the archaeologist has a unique understanding of tradition and custom, which is founded on the need to discover through physical evidence alone.

of a way of doing things that, firstly, has been going on for several generations and, secondly, cannot be done solely for some practical, functional reason or because of some external pressure.

It is with just these things that archaeologists identify cultural groups. It is only by the discovery of customs or traditions that cultural groups can be identified in pre-history. If everything found can be explained as a solely practical or functional response contingent upon something in the local environment, then there is nothing to identify a cultural group as something distinct.

Take, for example, the Beaker people: they are named after their beaker shaped pots and further identified by their decorated bowls and burial practices. These are all customs or traditions. The movement of these peoples in the second millennium BC from Spain to southern and western Europe and their assimilation with other peoples can be traced precisely by evidence of their customs and traditions.

From archaeologists, we can see that customs and traditions have to be something more than function or necessity. We can also see that they are a vital part of the cultural identity of a society or group. This can be observed today. To be Jewish is not only to believe in the one God of the scriptures, it is to live your life according to very specific traditions. These traditions may have been set down in holy scripture but Jewish theologians recognize that the practice of dietary laws, for example, do not make you a good person. But the practice of those laws is an important part of being Jewish. Tradition has been an essential factor in the survival of Judaism and the identity of the Jewish people through almost two millennia of persecution and dispersion.

We can learn more from the Jewish example. Not all Jewish tradition is ancient. The *Bar Mitzvah*, for example, is a German late medieval ceremony and it was only when Jews went to America that it became a big event. Adding to and inventing traditions like this is not just Jewish. It is quite common. The invention of tradition has a long and successful history: such as the invention of a codified tartan system in Scotland in the early nineteenth century and the flag folding ceremonies of the United States in the 1880s. In spite of their short history and deliberate concoction, these are still powerful symbols. Revealing their recent origins does not discredit them, it demonstrates their power.

The power of tradition in the bonding of social groups has for a long time been an important weapon in the armies of the world. In the little self-contained communities of regiments, traditions perform an essential function – they save lives. The creation of a dedicated social unit out of a random collection of recruits encourages soldiers to fight for one another. This is so successful that it is a common experience in battle for the soldier to have more sympathy with the enemy than with other friendly regiments.

As with many traditions, military traditions are generally ceremonial or based on obsolete functions. Peculiarities of parade drill or the wearing of obsolete weapons are common devices and are often knowingly invented. To be convincing, these traditions have to be based on the past. It does not matter if the past is real or fictional, it just has to be convincing. And yet for the military, more than any other profession, constant modernization is absolutely essential. The arms race is the most ruthless modernizer.

This marriage of change and tradition is found again and again. In times of change traditions are a source of stability. Change creates traditions. It can do this in two ways: by turning customs into traditions and by encouraging the invention of traditions. When a custom looks as if it is going to disappear, people suddenly discover it exists and often keep it going by turning it into a tradition. In the European Community today new regulations, which apply to several former nation states, have threatened a

Figure 3.3: The Talmud and Torah, symbols of Judaism, the great success story of traditional practice.

Figure 3.4: Regimental traditions, the deliberate preservation of obsolete weapons and historic uniforms to create social cohesion in a background of permanent modernization.

Figure 3.5: European harmonization is seen to dilute national identity by threatening national traditions. (Reproduced by kind permission of the Daily Mail*)*

Figure 3.6: Black Rod, a traditional ceremonial functionary who gives the impression of historic stability in a governmental system that is subject to radical change.

series of national customs. Suddenly aware of these customs, opponents of European harmonization have attacked the regulations and proposed that these customs be preserved to define individual national culture – in other words, they want to turn the customs into traditions.

Traditions are often invented or improved to protect changes or make them respectable. New nation states or political regimes in the last two centuries invented traditions to give an air of establishment to something quite new. In Germany, after unification in 1870, public holidays were established with elaborate ceremonies borrowed from Teutonic mythology. In the United States founding father mythologies were created, such the invention of the story of George Washington and the 'English cherry tree.'

The inventors of these traditions, consciously or unconsciously, looked for stability in tradition. Established systems were more attractive because they could create a firm background for radical change. A good example is the British parliamentary system. Parliament has existed for seven centuries and its method of operation is packed with traditional practices. These traditions create a strong sense of continuity. And yet, in a real political sense, the practice of obsolete functions is the only continuity. There is little practical resemblance between an occasional medieval advisory panel for monarchs and the body that fought the monarchy in the seventeenth century, or between the gerrymandering of the early nineteenth century and the universal suffrage of the twentieth century.

Tradition, therefore, is closely tied up with change – and modernization – in a number of different ways. This is not the dead hand of precedent or the laziness of habit. Far from being oppressive, tradition can be seen as positive social force, which bonds the community.

Tradition and architecture

The parallel with architecture is obvious. Our built surroundings, whether we like it or not, are part of our traditional culture. To destroy them is to destroy part of our culture. To deliberately destroy them or undermine them is to deliberately attack part of our culture.

It is not valid to claim to be part of a deeper or hidden tradition: if people cannot recognize it, then it is not a tradition at all. Nor is it valid to claim that the modern world makes all this obsolete, the need for traditions does not go away. If traditions cannot be found in something new they can be made up or borrowed. Early twentieth-century skyscrapers were Classical or Gothic. This was not just some fakery, the designers knew what they were doing, they just used tradition to make something new – just as architects had always done.

Figure 3.7: Christmas ceremonials are of great importance to family cohesion and cultural identity but often have false historical pedigrees.

The architectural preoccupation with the genuine does not fit this picture. It might be reassuring to know that a tradition is old but it does not matter very much. Knowing that Christmas trees were first introduced by Prince Albert in the nineteenth century does not stop us buying them. Everyone knows they are part of a tradition, they are not fakes or dishonest, they are traditional.

Figure 3.8: Sheriden House, Winchester by Robert Adam Architects.
Traditional design in an historic setting.

Conclusion

I can see nothing wrong and everything right about using obvious and understandable tradition in new design. I can see no good reason why being original is restricted to being non-traditional. I can see no good reason for saying that being creative means you cannot borrow things from the past – we all do it. I can see no good reason why new inventions have to look odd. Traditional design can be original, it can be creative and it can take on new things – it can even invent new traditions. If only we could all understand this, we could have a public that understands us, we could add to our historic culture instead of fighting it.

Section 2
The institutional and public perception

As we speed towards the end of the twentieth century and look back over developments in architecture and planning, the 1950s and 1960s are frequently cited, with some justification, as the years when most damage was done to towns and cities throughout Britain. Many areas had been severely damaged by war-time bombing and there was a need to rebuild quickly and a desire to sweep away the painful memories of the recent past. It is understandable perhaps that the architecture of the Modern Movement, which had gradually evolved between the wars in Europe, fitted perfectly with the vision for the future.

However, as Dennis Sharp points out in Section 1, by the 1950s, there was a wavering attitude towards certain aspects of the Modern Movement in Italy, where the architectural journals were making pronouncements against new buildings in historic settings, and in Britain The Architectural Review *took up its 'Townscape' campaign. Despite this, with the need to rebuild as quickly as possible, many architects took a more retrospective view and seized upon the pre-war ideas that seemed to provide the necessary answers to the problems of rebuilding for the future.*

Meanwhile, with their feet firmly on the ground, small groups of activists were gathering strength. Organisations such as The Civic Trust (founded 1957) and The Victorian Society (1958), could see historic buildings being destroyed without justification, and in 1967 the Civic Amenities Act brought protection in the form of conservation areas. From that time there has been increasing protection for the historic environment from amenity societies and government departments. Now, some would say that, whatever the motivation in the past, protection has gone too far and there is a danger of stifling the development of towns and cities for the future.

This section presents the perspective of some of those who have been charged with the unenviable responsibility of balancing the provision of new buildings with the protection of the historic environment. From the front line Mansell Jagger describes his approach to new development in the historic city of Canterbury and Les Sparks looks back over the post-war planning system and, through his experiences in Bath and Birmingham, shows how attitudes have gradually changed. Sherban Cantacuzino, formerly Secretary of The Royal Fine Art Commission, suggests how good buildings in historic settings might be achieved and Jukka Jokilheto provides an overview of world charters on the subject. From English Heritage Paul Velluet sets out current planning guidance and ends the section with his personal gazetteer of new buildings in historic settings.

Organizations, charters and world movements – an overview

Jukka Jokilehto Architect and Urban Planner

Summary

Since the 1933 Congrés Internationaux d'Architecture Moderne in Athens, which was mainly concerned with modern planning issues but did take into account the question of heritage in historic cities, there has been a wide range of charters, statements and management guidelines from several international organizations.

During the period after the First World War there was great influence from the Modern Movement, which was totally opposed to using past styles in contemporary buildings. After the Second World War, in some cites in Europe, there was a tendency to rebuild in styles that evoked the past although, in general, modern planning took precedence.

Historic urban areas received scant attention until 1965 with the foundation of the International Council on Monuments and Sites (ICOMOS), an international organization that was to take a firm lead in the protection of the historic fabric of cities. Following this several other organizations, including UNESCO, ICCROM, the Council of Europe, and in the USA the Secretary of the Interior have held seminars, conferences or issued guidelines on the subject.

In this chapter Jukka Jokilehto, an architect and urban planner who has been has been attached to ICCROM for almost twenty-five years, draws out those most relevant to new buildings in historic settings and shows how world attitudes have gradually changed.

Introduction

The issue of new buildings in historic settings emerged with the rise of modern technology and new urbanism in the nineteenth century. The conflict between the traditional town and modern development was denounced by A W N Pugin in 1836 in his book *Contrasts*, where he showed the difference between a 'Catholic town in 1440' and 'the same town in 1840': one with church steeples dominating the traditional townscape, and the other with modern multi-storey buildings and factory chimneys.[1] The problem of such modern 'invasion' was felt in several countries; for example, from the end of the nineteenth century German conservationists were writing in professional journals to debate the protection of historic townscapes.

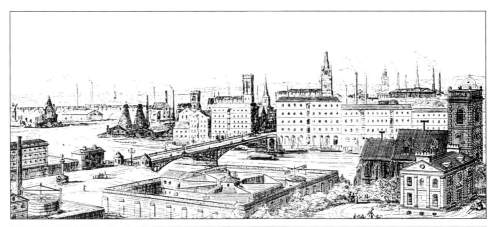

Figure 4.1: Catholic town in 1440 (bottom). The same town in 1840 (top). From A W N Pugin's 'Contrasts: or a parallel between the noble edifices of the Middle Ages and corresponding buildings of the present decay of taste'.

The influence of modernism in the inter-war period

As a result of the destruction caused by the First World War, there were some efforts to rebuild destroyed areas in old forms, such as at Arras in France and Louvain in Belgium. The supporters of the Modern Movement in architecture were, however, categorically and also 'morally' opposed to any imitation or the use of past styles in contemporary buildings. In this regard, Le Corbusier declared:

> The history of Architecture unfolds itself slowly across the centuries as a modification of structure and ornament, but in the last fifty years steel and concrete have brought new conquests, which are the index of a greater capacity for construction, and of an architecture in which the old codes have been overturned. If we challenge the past, we shall learn that 'styles' no longer exist for us, that a style belonging to our own period has come about; and there has been a revolution.[2]

This idea of an interruption between modern creativity and technology compared with the past was the dominant approach between the two world wars, and continued even later, although in parallel with other attitudes. In part, this approach also came from the growing conservation movement led by the philosophies of John Ruskin and William Morris, and the consciousness of historical authenticity that was more widely accepted in the first part of the twentieth century. The conclusions of the 1933 meeting in Athens, organized by the *Congrés Internationaux d'Architecture Moderne*, CIAM, were later published with the comments of Le Corbusier as *La Charte d'Athènes* (1941). The charter declared that,

Figure 4.2: The Renaissance square of Arras, France, rebuilt after destruction in the First World War.

'The use of past styles, with the pretext of aesthetics, has disastrous consequences in new constructions in historic zones. Continuing such habits, or introducing such initiatives will not be tolerated in any form.'[3] According to Le Corbusier, such methods would even be contrary to the lessons of history; a miserable copying of the past would be to jeopardize and discredit the real, authentic testimonies that merited preservation.

This same spirit was felt in the subsequent guidelines concerning the restoration of historic buildings adopted by the Italian Ministry of Education in 1938. Coherent with the policy of the previous charters by Camillo Boito (1883) and Gustavo Giovannoni (1931–32), the Italian guidelines emphasized that eventual additions to or the replacement of elements in historic monuments should be made in simple architectural forms using materials and techniques that clearly had the mark of modernity, as well as avoiding any decorative or figurative reproduction. Concerning historic areas, every effort should be made to maintain existing historic fabric intact. In cases where historic buildings had remained isolated, their surroundings should be built 'in absolute neutrality regarding spaces and elevations', as well as avoiding any involvement of generically monumental or scenographic arrangements.[4]

The need for historicism

The massive destruction during the Second World War provoked strong feelings towards the past and, although modern planning and building became the rule of the day, there were several cases where the question of the integrity of historic surroundings had to be taken into serious consideration. Apart form some large-scale reconstruction, such as in Warsaw, or large-scale renewals, such as London, there were many cases where intermediate solutions were sought. The purpose was to recall some memories from the past and to find solutions where new construction would adhere to the scale and general character of an historic area. In the centre of Florence the destroyed buildings on the Arno River were rebuilt in modern forms, which reflected similar articulation to the existing building fronts.

A wide range of such solutions was developed in sectors of Germany. For example, in the German Democratic Republic, some monumental ensembles of Dresden were left in ruins (e.g. the Royal castle and Frauenkirche) in view of their eventual restoration or reconstruction later, while the general line was to respect modernity not only in new constructions, but also in the form of the newly designed parts of the city. In the case of Hildesheim, West Germany, the destroyed city was rebuilt maintaining the historic street pattern and scale, but using modern forms in the new buildings (*Figures 4.3 & 4.4*). It is interesting to note that the central square of the town has since been rebuilt a second time (in the 1980s), and now is a replica of its pre-war situation, which reflects the citizens' request for a 'memorial'.

By contrast, the destroyed centre of Nuremberg was rebuilt by adopting some general characteristics of the lost urban fabric, for example using similar materials (such as sandstone) and similar features, but solving the technical details with a clearly modern flavour (*Figure 4.5*). In both cases, ruined churches and some important monuments were rebuilt and restored. The general purpose was to retain the memory of the place and to give continuity to the history of the town.

In 1962 France adopted the so-called *Loi Malraux*, a law concerned to safeguard protected areas, proposed by the Minister of Culture, André Malraux. This was the first such law in Europe, and it became a reference for other countries. The law encouraged collaboration of architects responsible for historic buildings with the Ministry of Town Planning and politicians. The purpose, at the beginning, was to select derelict, picturesque areas, and to practically rebuild them as 'monumental areas' to demonstrate their architectural and aesthetic qualities. It resulted in policies reminiscent of nineteenth-century 'stylistic restoration'. The first attempts were considered a failure and it took a radical change in implementation policies to achieve acceptable results in the 1980s.[5] One of the problems had certainly been the lack of consideration of the needs and values of the

Figure 4.3: The historic town of Hildesheim rebuilt after destruction in the Second World War. The new buildings correspond to the design of the period (1950s) but the old street lines are maintained.

Figure 4.4: The central square of Hildesheim rebuilt in the 1980s replacing the post-war buildings with replicas of the historic structures destroyed in the Second World War.

inhabitants. It is perhaps not by chance that Henri Lefebre stressed the citizens' right to the city (*Le Droit à la ville*, Paris 1968), and analysed the results of city planning in the hands of different interest groups: people of good will (such as architects and writers) who may not have realized that human scale had changed from the traditional to modern society, state administrators who aimed at a global system, or property developers who were principally market oriented.

In various countries, guidelines were developed for the control of new constructions in historic settings. In France, such guidelines stressed the use of traditional materials and characteristic architectural forms and details especially in rural areas. In the United States, the well-known Secretary of the Interior's *Standards for the Treatment of Historic Properties* and the *Guidelines for Preserving, Rehabilitating, Restoring & Reconstructing Historic Buildings* (1978)[6] do not specifically speak about modern architecture in historic settings. However, the standards require that 'a reconstruction will be clearly identified as a contemporary re-creation'.[7] The guidelines specify that reconstruction should not be undertaken unless based on sufficient research, nor giving an historic site 'a false appearance by basing the reconstruction or conjectural designs or the availability of features

Figure 4.5: The reconstruction of the historic area of Nuremberg was inspired by historic forms and materials.

from other nearby sites'.[8] Furthermore, structures 'confusing the historic spatial relationship between buildings and landscape features within the setting by reconstructing some missing elements, but not others' are discouraged.[9]

In Italy, the planning policies of historic towns evolved since the 1960s. The plans of Assisi, Gubbio and Vincenza were the first where the historic centre was considered an integral whole, but importance was still given mainly on historic monuments. In the late 1960s and early 1970s, in the examples of Urbino and Rimini (Giancarlo De Carlo), the idea was to pre-design the appearance of new constructions, obliging them to harmonize with the character of the historic city – as the princes had done in the past (*Figures 4.6 & 4.7*). Care was taken to guarantee the relationship of the historic town with its surrounding landscape, although limited areas outside the historic walls of the city were reserved for modern housing development. At the same time, Bologna, Brescia and Ferrara took a different approach, and the conservation plan was undertaken by a team within the city administration. The purpose was to identify the typology of the buildings and spaces in historic areas, and to integrate these with the social and economic policies addressing the needs of the citizens. New buildings were designed to respect the typology of the historic fabric, but were modern in their details and architectural interpretation. However, policies could vary from one city to another; Bologna applied more strictly the concept of typology, while Ferrara gave more freedom to contemporary expression.[10] It was characteristic of such policies not to limit the planning methods to the historic centre area, but to consider historical the entire municipal territory. The purpose was to reach a balanced distribution of services, but also to use the same type of planning process in each part of the city, including areas reserved for agriculture and industry.

Figure 4.6: In the plan of Urbino, the historic character of the place and the traditional materials of house fronts and street pavings were respected in providing models for eventual in-fill buildings.

The foundation of ICOMOS

Although the question of historic towns was discussed at the Venice meeting in 1964, the Venice Charter itself did not enter into the merits of city planning. Instead, the International Council on Monuments and Sites, ICOMOS, founded in 1965, generated an increasing number of national and international conferences and symposia with recommendations and statements related to such problems. Within ICOMOS, the concern for historic cities was principally assumed by the International Committee on Historic Cities and Villages, CIVVIH, who have since collaborated in a number of such declarations. As a result of a meeting in Bruges in 1975, the *Principles governing the rehabilitation of historic towns* recognized that preservation necessi-

Figure 4.7: The conservation plan of Bologna became a classic example in the 1970s for the reintegration of areas where the historic urban fabric had been lost. The idea was to base the new design (in the photograph) on the characteristic features of the building types in the area concerned.

tated the adaptation of historic towns to the requirements of contemporary life, but that this should be done without destroying its existing fabric, structure, or historical evidence. The principles also accepted the possibility of new buildings in historic settings; it declared that respect for authenticity implied the integration of modern architecture in old towns *(paragraph 10)*. This meant that importance was given to functional continuity as well as maintenance of historic fabric. Following the same lines of thought, the 1987 ICOMOS Charter for the Conservation of Historic Towns and Urban Areas declared *(article 10)*:

> When it is necessary to construct new buildings or adapt existing ones, the existing spatial layout should be respected, especially in terms of scale and lot size. The introduction of contemporary elements in harmony with the surroundings should not be discouraged since such features can contribute to the enrichment of an area.

European Charters

The year 1975 was declared the European Architectural Heritage Year by the Council of Europe, and several conferences were organized in its Member States. In September, the European Committee of Ministers adopted the *European Charter of the Architectural Heritage*, which emphasized the need to guarantee a harmonious social balance in historic cities. The charter also defined the concept of 'integrated conservation', and referring to new buildings, it declared:

> It should be noted that integrated conservation does not rule out the introduction of modern architecture into areas containing old buildings provided that the existing context, proportions, forms, sizes and scale are fully respected and traditional materials are used. *(article 7)*

The Heritage Year concluded with the *Amsterdam Declaration* resulting from a conference in October 1975. The declaration stressed legal, administrative, social, economic and educational issues in safeguarding historic areas. Special attention was given to the specificity of each urban area, the need to respect such characteristics 'intelligently, sensitively and with economy', and to ensure 'that traditional building materials remain available and that traditional crafts and techniques continue to be used.' The same concepts were promoted in the *Convention for the Protection of the Architectural Heritage of Europe*, Granada 1985, which emphasized that integrated conservation policies should:

> include the protection of architectural heritage as an essential town and country planning objective and ensure that this requirement is taken into account at all stages both in the drawing up of development plans and in the procedures for authorizing work. *(article 10)*

The influence of UNESCO and ICCROM

In 1976, the Member States of UNESCO adopted the *Recommendation Concerning the Safeguarding and Contemporary Role of Historic Areas*. Particular emphasis was given to the idea that historic areas and their surroundings were composed not only of the physical parts but also of human activities that together formed a coherent whole. It was this 'integrity' that should be understood and safeguarded in the process of any modern development and 'great attention should be paid to the harmony and aesthetic feeling produced by the linking and contrasting of the various parts which make up the groups of buildings and which give to each group its particular character.' *(article 4)* Any modern constructions in the immediate surroundings should be so designed as to 'ensure that views from and to monuments and historic areas are not spoilt and that historic areas are integrated harmoniously into contemporary life.' *(article 5)*

In the context of the 1972 UNESCO *World Heritage Convention*, historic towns have gained particular importance, and increasing attention is given to defining the nominations in a more comprehensive way. One of the principal requirements for including a cultural heritage resource on the list of World Heritage sites is that it should 'pass the test of authenticity'. In the case of historic cities, this requirement has not been easy to apply. Attention has been given to the verification of the historic fabric of cities, ensuring that modern interventions have not seriously modified such features. The convention itself does not specify policies related to new constructions. However, in this context, the *Management Guidelines for World Cultural Heritage Sites*, published by ICCROM,[11] emphasize that the primary objective of conservation planning is the conservation of existing historic fabric:

> The building of new structures should not be an excuse for demolishing old ones. New construction may, however, be necessary to re-establish functional and architectural continuity, and in cases where empty lots might be hazardous to or further decay surrounding buildings.[12]

It is possible to identify design criteria related to architectural requirements, but it is equally essential to consider the historical integrity of an historic settlement. This demands identification of the elements that together define the fabric and infrastructures of a city, their mutual connections, and the relationship within the cultural landscape of which the settlement is part. Policies regarding the construction of new buildings should be based on the understanding of these complex relationships.

Conclusion

Taking a simplified view on historic city centres, two approaches can be identified, one aimed at conservation, the other aimed at innovation. In 1934, Luigi Piccinato described these approaches by stating that, while conservators gave priority to preserving the architectural features of the buildings, this easily led to innovation by introducing new functions, such as those related to tourism and museums, and the removal of traditional uses from the area. On the other hand, innovators, while causing radical changes by building new structures, were conservative in keeping the functions of the city centre.[13] This comparison is clearly exaggerated but behind it there lies some serious thought. As the various international recommendations have emphasized, an essential part of the historic city is its function as an urban ensemble. Although tourism is certainly one of the principal economic forces in modern world, it provides a challenge that is not easy to meet. The risk is to substitute the identity of an historic town with that of a tourist centre, which can easily lead to *kitsch* and be destructive. It can be noted that, since the Modern Movement evolved into Post-Modernism, the amount of new design in historical styles, as well as the reconstruction of destroyed historic buildings, has certainly increased. Such development is not encouraged by official statements in international guidelines or charters – although it can be tolerated under specified conditions.

The ICCROM *Management Guidelines* emphasize: 'One of the objects of urban conservation is to control the rate of change in the urban system. We therefore need to comprehend the life forces of that system and the potential causes of its decay.'[14] There is a fundamental need to identify and strike a balance between different types of values – those related to historic ensembles and those related to current needs – and to guarantee sustainable human and environmental development of such communities.[15] This requirement was clearly recognized in international conferences such as the Habitat II conference in Istanbul in 1996. Concerning the policies related to new buildings in historic settings, the international guidelines generally recognize that this can be feasible under specific conditions. Conservation theorists can accept the principle of creative contributions of all ages as part of the historical continuum, but this cannot be taken as a rule; the specificity and the integrity of each place need to be taken into account. Furthermore, new additions should not be an excuse for the demolition of existing historic fabric, they should not falsify the historical, architectural and functional character of the place.

References:

1 PUGIN, A W N, *Contrasts*, Leicester University Press, New York, 1973, p.105 (first published in 1836).

2 LE CORBUSIER, *Towards a New Architecture*, The Architectural Press, 1927 (reprinted 1976), p. 13.

3 LE CORBUSIER, *La Charte d'Athènes*, Èditions de Minuit, Paris, 1957, p.91.

4 ROME, Ministero della Pubblica Istruzione 'Istruzioni per il restauro dei monumenti' 1938. In: G Monti, *La conservazione dei beni culturali nei documenti italiani e internazionali, 1931–1991*, Ministero per i Beni Culturali e Ambientali, Ufficio Studi, Istituto Poligrafico e Zecca dello Stato, Roma, 1995, pp.34–35.

5 HOULET, Jacques, 'Vingt ans d'application de la Loi Malraux sur les secteurs sauvegardés' In: ICOMOS, 1993 *Conservación de ciudades, pueblos y barrios históricas*, Revista Científica ICOMOS 2, CIVVIH, Xunta de Galicia, 1993, pp.240–265.

6 USA, *The Secretary of the Interior's Standards for the Treatment of Historic Properties with Guidelines for Preserving, Rehabilitating, Restoring & Reconstructing Historic Buildings*, by Kay D. Weeks and Anne E. Grimmer, U.S.

Department of the Interior, National Parks Service, Washington, D.C. 1995.

7   *Ibid*. p.166.

8   *Ibid*. p.174.

9   *Ibid*. p.175.

10 CESARI, C, 'El proceso de conservación y rehabilitación en Italia' In: ICOMOS, 1993. *Conservación de ciudades, pueblos y barrios históricas*, Revista Científica ICOMOS 2, CIVVIH, Xunta de Galicia, 1993 pp.278–290.

11 FEILDEN, B M & JOKILEHTO, J, *Management Guidelines for World Cultural Heritage Sites*, ICCROM, Rome, 1993.

12 *Ibid*. pp.91ff.

13 STOCKEL, G, 'Risanamento e demolizioni nel tessuto delle città italiane negli anni trenta'. In: G Bozzoni, G Carbonara, G Villetti, eds. *Saggi in onore di Renato Bonelli*, Quaderni dell'Istituto di Stori di Architettura, Università degli Studi, Roma, 1992, pp.859ff.

14 FEILDEN, B M & JOKILEHTO, J, *op.cit* p.82.

15 ZANCHETI, Silvio M, & JOKILEHTO, J, 'Values and urban conservation planning: some reflections on principles and definitions', *Journal of Architectural Conservation*, No.1, Vol.3, March 1997.

Further reading

JOKILEHTO, J, 'International standards, principles and charters of conservation'. In: S Marks, ed. *Concerning Buildings, Studies in Honour of Sir Bernard Feilden*, Butterworth-Heinemann, Oxford, 1996, pp.55–81.

UNESCO, *Conventions and Recommendations of Unesco concerning the Protection of the Cultural Heritage, Paris*, 1985.

The national interest

5

Paul Velluet English Heritage

Summary

Historic buildings, including both those created in the vernacular tradition and those designed formally, are valued for a variety of reasons not least because of their contribution to the cultural identity of the nation.

Despite concern for the protection of the historic environment, which can be traced back centuries from a number of individuals and groups, the first formal system for the designation and protection of conservation areas came into effect under the Civic Amenities Act, 1967. Since then, the planning control system has been developed to try to ensure that the many historic buildings and areas throughout the country have been conserved rather than lost or damaged and that new development in these areas is sensitive to its historic environment.

Some say that conservation has gone too far and controls are excessive, however, with new development there is plenty of encouragement for creativity and innovation. As the discussion document 'Quality in Town and Country', July 1994 states, '.... We should ensure that the planning system does not stifle responsible innovation and originality.'

In this chapter, Paul Velluet, Head of the Central and West London Team and Regional Architect, English Heritage, London Region sifts through the myriad of statutory controls and guidance notes to highlight the relevant sections on development in historic areas. He sets out the guidance on the subject from local authorities, central government, and English Heritage. Along the way he underlines the importance of an enlightened patron and concludes by suggesting his own criterion for new buildings in historic settings.

Introduction

For centuries, an innate and deep understanding of regional or local building traditions and their effective application and development informed the design and construction of the majority of the country's vernacular buildings and structures. Similarly, an appreciation for such traditions, together with a regard for context and a desire for civility and literacy in architecture, influenced the design and construction of diverse formal buildings and structures. Such buildings and structures, where they continue to survive in settlements, both urban and rural, are frequently valued both locally and nationally not only for their particular historic or architectural interest but because of the considerable contribution they make to the local scene and to the cultural continuity of local communities.

Despite the immense changes to the structure and nature of society resulting from the Industrial Revolution and urbanization during the nineteenth century and from the vast social and technological changes of the present century, the relevance of those factors that shaped so much of our built environment in past centuries remains undiminished.

In the opening paragraph of its formal guidance on planning and the historic environment, central government rightly stresses the fundamental relevance of the effective protection for all aspects of the historic environment to its policies for environmental stewardship:

> The physical survivals of our past are to be valued and protected for their own sake, as a central part of our cultural heritage and our sense of national identity. They are an irreplaceable record which contributes, through formal education and in many other ways, to our understanding of both the present and the past. Their presence adds to the quality of our lives, by enhancing the familiar and cherished local scene and sustaining the sense of local distinctiveness which is so important an aspect of our towns, villages and countrywide. The historic environment is also of immense importance for leisure and recreation. (*Planning Policy Guidance: Planning and the historic environment [PPG15]*, September 1994: paragraph 1.1)

However, central government also rightly and commendably stresses its concerns about the value and quality of new development:

> Preservation is not enough. What we build today will have an important impact upon future generations, and every new building influences how we feel about a place or street. That puts a high value on good design whether we are building in town or country .... Prima facie, to build ought to be to improve .... Good architecture need not be more expensive, nor need it be more difficult to realise. Yet in contributes hugely to the regeneration of our towns and cities. With imagination, creativity and sensitivity we can provide quality at reasonable cost .... A new building is rarely viewed in isolation: people both see and use a building in context. It is important that new development recognises that context, which may mean the immediate neighbours, the

street or square, as the building traditions of the wider area. Successful new buildings are often those that unselfishly integrate into their context, borrowing from local building techniques and using local materials. Yet these are always instances where something different is required. We should ensure that the planning system does not stifle responsible innovation and originality. (*Quality in Town and Country: A Discussion Document*, July, 1994: p14)

Such attitudes and aspirations clearly lead to the need to balance the interests of preservation and new development intelligently and with discernment, and such an objective clearly requires control systems based upon policies and their application characterised by reasonableness, flexibility and consistency.

Responsibility for the historic environment

It is frequently argued today in certain very specific areas of the architectural, building and development press and in some architectural and development circles that conservation has gone too far and that planning and related controls are excessive, exclusively negative and counterproductive in their effect. However, such views would seem to be largely inconsistent with the reality of the vast improvements in the character and quality of new development relating to both historic buildings and historic areas evident over the last thirty years; throughout the greater part of the country, coinciding with increasing awareness and legislation relating to the protection of the historic environment, with the increasing emphasis on quality and sensitivity in design in the planning system, and with the increased role of public participation in that system. In this connection, it is worth observing that the system for the designation and protection of conservation areas first came into effect in 1967 (under the *Civic Amenities Act, 1967*), that the present system for the control of works to listed buildings came into effect in 1968 (under the *Town and Country Planning Act 1968,* and that the immensely important Skeffington Report on public participation in the planning process (*People and Planning: Report of the Committee on Public Participation in Planning*), was published in 1969. Whilst it would be absurd to suggest that such improvements were wholly attributable to the planning and related control systems, or that such systems have worked perfectly over that most significant period, the present control systems that have been put in place and developed between 1967 and 1997 have clearly had a major and beneficial effect in ensuring that countless historic buildings and areas throughout the country have been effectively conserved rather than lost or irredeemably damaged, and that for the most part, there has been a marked improvement in the quality and sensitivity of new development in historic settings.

Whilst it is obvious that the present planning and related control systems cannot guarantee excellence in terms of quality of new design, they can, when soundly and intelligently administered by local planning authorities, provide a climate in which sensitivity and quality in the design of new buildings in historic settings can be nurtured and sustained. In such a climate, therefore, whilst the risk of mediocrity cannot be wholly ruled out due to the limitations arising from the courts' interpretation of existing statutory provisions, there is no reason why excellence cannot be encouraged and achieved. As is increasingly obvious to so many, it is in the exercise of enlightened patronage in the commissioning of new buildings and in the allocation of appropriate levels of resources to effect their realization that architectural excellence is more likely to be reached.

The power of local authorities

Turning to the specific powers available to local planning authorities in controlling new development affecting historic buildings and areas, it is pertinent to refer to the basic statutory provisions:

> In considering whether to grant planning permission for development which affects a listed building or its setting, the local planning authority or, as the case may be, the Secretary of State shall have special regard to the desirability of preserving the building or its setting or any features of special architectural or historic interest which it possesses. (*The Planning [Listed Buildings and Conservation Areas] Act, 1990*, Section 66)

> In the exercise, with respect to any buildings or other land in a conservation area, of any powers under any of the provisions .... special attention shall be paid to the desirability of preserving or enhancing the character or appearance of that area.
> (*The Planning [Listed Buildings and Conservation Areas] Act, 1990*, Section 72)

In other words, in looking at proposals for new development in a historic setting, local planning authorities are formally required to have 'special regard' to the desirability of 'preserving' a listed building or its setting, or any features of special interest which it possesses and to give 'special attention' to the desirability of 'preserving or enhancing' the character or appearance of a conservation area. However, in the light of the judgement in the South Lakeland case,[1] although the opportunity to enhance an area through a new development may well be viewed as a reasonable and desirable objective by a local authority, the failure of a scheme to provide for such enhancement or positive preservation cannot in itself be regarded as a justification for resisting the proposal providing that the scheme would leave the character and appearance of the area unharmed; i.e. is by maintaining the status quo. Here then, is the potential 'mediocrity factor', for it is clear that the power of local authorities is effectively limited to resisting only those developments which could be reasonably regarded as failing to preserve a listed building or its setting, or the character or appearance of a conservation area. Such a constraint, therefore, precludes local planning authorities from securing anything more than satisfactory solutions through the threat of withholding formal approval. Accordingly, to secure higher standards requires a more distinctly positive and creative approach on the part of local planning authorities, extending the 'regulatory' role to a more 'proactive' or collaborative role; seeking an effective 'partnership' with prospective developers and their designers. An obvious lever available to planning authorities in this context is the assurance of a speedy and positive outcome to the application process if a prospective developer offers a scheme of a quality and sensitivity that rises above the level of mere acceptability.

Central government advice

Encouragingly, current formal advice from central government makes specific reference to the desirability of 'good' design, rightly stressing that:

> Good design should be the aim of all those involved in the development process and should be encouraged everywhere. Good design can help promote sustainable development, improve the quality of the existing environment, attract business and investment; and reinforce civic pride and a sense of place. It can help to secure continued public acceptance of necessary new development.

> Applicants for planning permission should be able to demonstrate how they have taken account of the need for good design in their development proposals and that they have had regard to relevant development plan policies and supplementary design guidance. This should be done in a manner appropriate to the nature and scale of the proposals. (*Planning Policy Guidance: General Policy and Principles, [PPG1] [revised]*, February 1997, paragraphs 15 and 16)

Such advice is set out further to more general advice on the design of development in *PPG1 [revised]*.

> New buildings and their curtilages have a significant effect on the character and quality of an area. They define public spaces, streets and vistas and inevitably create the context for future development. These effects will often be to the benefit of an area but they can be detrimental. They are matters of proper public interest. The appearance of proposed development and its relationship to its surroundings are therefore material considerations in determining planning applications and appeals. Such considerations relate to the design of buildings and to urban design. These are distinct, albeit closely interrelated subjects. Both are important. Both require an understanding of the context in which development takes place whether in urban or rural areas.

> Local planning authorities should reject poor designs, particularly where their decisions are supported by clear plan policies or supplementary design guidance

which has been subjected to public consultation and adopted by the local planning authority. Poor designs may include those inappropriate to their context, for example those clearly not of scale or incompatible with their surroundings.

Local planning authorities should not attempt to impose a particular architectural taste or style arbitrarily. It is, however, proper to seek to promote or reinforce local distinctiveness particularly where this is supported by clear plan policies or supplementary design guidance. Local planning authorities should not concern themselves with matters of detailed design except where such matters have a significant effect on the character or quality of the area, including neighbouring buildings. Particular weight should be given to the impact of development on existing buildings and on the character of areas recognized for their landscape or townscape value, such as National Parks, Areas of Outstanding Natural Beauty and Conservation Areas.

Where the design of proposed development is consistent with relevant design policies and supplementary design guidance, planning permission should not be refused on design grounds unless there are exceptional circumstances. Design policies and guidance should focus on encouraging good design and should avoid stifling responsible innovation, originality or initiative. Such policies and guidance should recognize that the qualities of an outstanding scheme may exceptionally justify departing from them. (*PPG 1 [revised]* paragraphs 13, 17, 18 and 19)

Commendably, for the first time in any formal advice issued by central government, *PPG1 [revised]* refers specifically to 'urban design' and offers both a definition and relevant guidance:

For the purposes of this Guidance, urban design should be taken to mean the relationship between different buildings; the relationship between buildings and the streets, squares, parks, waterways and other spaces which make up the public domain; the nature and quality of the public domain itself; the relationship of one part of a village, town or city with other parts; and the patterns of movement and activity which are thereby established; in short, the complex relationships between all the elements of built and unbuilt space. As the appearance and treatment of the spaces between and around buildings is often of comparable importance to the design of the buildings themselves, landscape design should be considered as an integral part of urban design. (*PPG1 [revised]*, paragraph 14)

Finally, Annex A of *PPG1 [revised]* contains further guidance on the expression of design policies in development plans and supplementary design guidance, and on the information relating to design which should be submitted with planning applications. Such advice is relevant, positive, and entirely unobjectionable and can only serve to encourage improved sensitivity and quality in the design of new development, not least through its specific exhortation that illustrative material supporting planning applications 'should show the wider context and not just the development site and its immediately adjacent buildings.'

Central government's most relevant advice on the design of new buildings in historic areas is contained in *Planning Policy Guidance: Planning and the historic environment (PPG 15)* issued in September 1994:

> The design of new buildings intended to stand alongside historic buildings needs very careful consideration. In general it is better that old buildings are not set apart, but are woven into the fabric of the living and working community. This can be done, provided that the new buildings are carefully designed to respect their setting, follow fundamental architectural principles of scale, height, massing and alignment, and use appropriate materials. This does not mean that new buildings have to copy their older neighbours in detail: some of the most interesting streets in our towns and villages include a variety of building styles, materials and forms of construction, of many different periods, but together forming a harmonious group .... (*PPG 15*, paragraph 2.14)

In referring to the statutory obligation placed upon local planning authorities to have regard to the potential impact of new development on the setting of a listed building, the formal guidance quite properly stresses that:

> .... the setting is often an essential part of the building's character, especially if a garden or grounds have been laid out to complement its design or function. Also, the economic viability as well as the character of historic buildings may suffer and they can be robbed of much of their interest, and of the contribution they make to townscape or the countryside, if they become isolated from their surroundings, e.g. by new traffic routes, car parks, or other development.

> .... the setting of a building may be limited to obviously ancillary land, but may often include land some distance from it. Even where a building has no ancillary land – for example in a crowded urban street – the setting may encompass a number of other properties. The setting of individual listed buildings very often owes its character to the harmony produced by a particular grouping of buildings (not necessarily all of great individual merit) and to the quality of the spaces created between them. Such areas require careful appraisal when proposals for development are under consideration, even if the redevelopment would only replace a building which is neither itself listed nor immediately adjacent to a listed building. Where a listed building forms an important visual element in a street, it would probably be right to regard any development in the street as being within the setting of the building. A proposed high or bulky building might also affect the setting of a listed building some distance away, or alter views of a historic skyline. In some cases, setting can only be defined by a historical assessment of a building's surroundings. If there is doubt about the precise extent of a building's setting, it is better to publish a notice. (*PPG 15*, paragraphs 2.16 and 2.17)

PPG 15 also contains central government's formal advice on the control of development within conservation areas:

> Many conservation areas include the commercial centres of the towns and villages of which they form part. While conservation (whether by preservation or enhancement) of their character or appearance must be a major consideration, this cannot realistically take the form of preventing all new development; the emphasis will generally need to be on controlled and positive management of change. Policies will need to be designed to allow the area to remain alive and prosperous, and to avoid unnecessarily detailed controls over businesses and householders, but at the same time to ensure that any new development accords with the area's special architectural and historic interest.
>
> Many conservation areas include gap sites, or buildings that make no positive contribution to, or indeed detract from, the character or appearance of the area; their replacement should be a stimulus to imaginative, high quality design, and seen as an opportunity to enhance the area. What is important is not that new buildings should directly imitate earlier styles, but that they should be designed with respect for their context, as part of a larger whole which has a well-established character and appearance of its own.
>
> Local planning authorities will often need to ask for detailed plans and drawings of proposed new development, including elevations which show the new development in its setting, before considering a planning application. In addition to adopted local plan policies, it may be helpful to prepare design briefs for individually important 'opportunity' sites. Special regard should be had for such matters as scale, height, form, massing, respect for the traditional pattern of frontages, vertical or horizontal emphasis and detailed design (e.g. the scale and spacing of window openings, and the nature and quality of materials). General planning standards should be applied sensitively in the interests of harmonizing the new development with its neighbours in the conservation area. (*PPG 15*, paragraphs 4.16, 17 and 18)

The role of English Heritage

Over recent years, English Heritage has taken an increasing interest in the issue of new development in the historic environment; stemming not only from its continuing role as a formal consultee for planning applications relating to certain categories of development affecting listed buildings and conservation areas (and registered parks and gardens), but from a growing awareness of the crucial importance of the location, nature and design of new buildings, structures and other developments to the future survival of the character and appearance of historic settlements throughout the country, whether villages, towns or cities.

Such interest has been reflected in the publication of a number of important advice documents:

- *Conservation issues in strategic plans*, published jointly by English Heritage, English Nature and the Countryside Commission in 1993

- *Conservation in London: A study of strategic planning policy in London*, published jointly by English Heritage and the London Planning Advisory Committee in January 1995

- *Development in the historic environment: An English Heritage guide to policy, procedure and good practice*, published in June 1995

- *Conservation Area Practice: English Heritage guidance on the management of conservation areas*, published in October 1995

- *Conservation issues in local plans*, published jointly by English Heritage, English Nature and the Countryside Commission in 1996

Of particular relevance is the guidance contained in *Conservation Area Practice* at paragraph 8.3 on the design of new buildings in historic areas:

> In considering proposals for new buildings in conservation areas the principal concerns should be the appropriateness of the overall mass or volume of the building, its scale (the expression of size indicated by the windows, doors, floor heights, and other identifiable units), and its relationship with its context – whether it sits comfortably. A new building should be in harmony with, or complementary to, its neighbours, having regard to the pattern, rhythms, and details of the adjoining buildings, and especially their architectural style. The use of materials generally matching those which are historically dominant in the areas is important, as is the need for the development not to have a visually disruptive impact on the existing townscape or street scene. It should also, as far as possible, fit into the 'grain' of an historic area, for example by respecting surviving medieval street patterns. All these aspects can be assessed to a large degree without reference to the architectural style adopted for the design, whether contemporary or historicist. The few exceptions will include new development forming part of, or adjoining, an important architectural set piece of recognized quality, which must be taken into account.

In addition, and of particular significance, has been English Heritage's important role in the discussions and deliberations relating to a range of major urban conservation and development proposals in major cities and towns; working closely with relevant local planning authorities and other bodies, such as the Royal Fine Art Commission. In an increasing number of cases, English Heritage has sought to encourage more confident contemporary architectural solutions rather than unduly restrained or conservative designs.

However, it is only by assessing the effectiveness of policies and guidance and their application in practice that the benefits accruing from the highly developed planning and conservation legislation existing in this country today can be properly evaluated. In this connection, it is clearly necessary to look at and judge an extensive and diverse range of relevant projects completed in recent years or nearing completion today. It is to be hoped that an increasing number of projects should reflect the results of sound and intelligent application of the planning control system and the increase of enlightened patronage by building owners and developers. Some are listed in Chapter 9.

Conclusion

A regard for context and an understanding and appreciation of the past need pose no threat to architectural creativity or excellence. In some cases there may be a need for reticence or deference, but this need not lead to mediocrity or banality. In many cases a new building can make a positive and distinct contribution to its setting, enhancing the character and appearance of the area in which it is located. Similarly, whilst the design of some new buildings may draw explicit influence from historical sources, either formal or vernacular, this need not lead to 'pastiche' or 'historicist' solutions in their pejorative senses.

In his excellent study: *What Makes a Good Building? An inquiry by the Royal Fine Art Commission,*[2] Sherban Cantacuzino put forward six 'criteria' relevant to successful design: order and unity; expression; integrity; plan and section; detail; and integration. In relation to the sixth criterion, he suggested that there were at least six qualities that a building needed to fit into its surroundings harmoniously; namely appropriate siting, massing, scale, proportion, rhythm and materials.

However, it is perhaps apposite to conclude by quoting from Sir Henry Wotton's *Elements of Architecture*, 1624[3]:

> In Architecture as in all other operative Arts, the end must direct the Operation. The end is to build well. Well building hath three conditions. Commodity, Firmness and Delight.

It is reasonable to suggest that the quality of 'delight' should be as important a factor in the consideration of context as it is in that of architecture.

References
1 SOUTH LAKELAND DC v Secretary of State for the Environment [1992] 2 WLR 204.
2 CANTACUZINO, S, *What Makes a Good Building? An inquiry by the Royal Fine Art Commission,* The Royal Fine Art Commission, 1994.
3 WOTTON, Sir Henry, *Elements of Architecture,* 1624.

Historicism and the public perception

Les Sparks *Director of Planning and Architecture Birmingham City Council*

Summary

The second half of the twentieth century has seen a shifting focus of power over the control of our historic environment. Until the end of the nineteenth century control rested with the landlord. It was not until between the wars that the issue of historic building destruction became a concern. The 1947 Town and Country Planning Act introduced lists of buildings that were worthy of preservation, with the result that the freedom of property owners was curtailed. Power shifted to the developer and public authority in partnership, who behind closed doors masterminded the wholesale redevelopment of urban centres. The 1950s and early 1960s provided architects with the opportunity to introduce modern architecture to Britain on an unprecedented scale.

Comprehensive redevelopment and the 'brave new world' of modern architecture led to the public protest campaigns of the 1970s. The Skeffington Report on public participation shifted power to local councillors, residents and community organizations. The proliferation of residents' associations, conservation committees and amenity societies brought a third force into planning, with the emphasis on retention rather than development.

Architecture and the quality of the environment was no longer the sole perogative of the professionals. Journalists and historians led the way in a counter-view on urban values. The pendulum had swung full distance but there was none-the-less a dichotomy for the general public who required effectiveness and efficiency, which is frequently in conflict with old buildings. This has often resulted in either façadism or creating new buildings in historical styles.

The power of public concern is to be applauded but it should not be power without responsibility for the underlying issues. We are perhaps now at a stage when local groups will come together with owners, developers, public authorities and designers to 'produce buildings that are recognizably of our own age but with an understanding and respect for history and context.'

Changing attitudes towards historic buildings

The second half of the twentieth century has seen an increasing tussle for control over the environment. Power has continuously shifted between the different professions, landowners, developers, politicians and bureaucrats. This has significantly determined the fate of our towns and cities – including some of the most historic places in Europe.

Until the late nineteenth century, control rested with the landowner. Patron and designer built according to the very latest architectural fashions and techniques. New architectural styles were introduced alongside earlier ones without hindrance or hesitation. Older buildings were replaced, apparently without concern. Nineteenth-century bylaws, introduced to control the excesses of speculators and profiteers, were only concerned with health and hygiene, drainage, fresh air and sound structures. Concern over the destruction of old buildings eventually emerged as an issue between the two world wars. The year 1937 saw both the introduction of The Bath Corporation Act and the formation of the campaigning organization The Georgian Group, which were both concerned with the preservation of eighteenth-century architecture that was particularly unfashionable and under threat at the time.

Figure 6.1: Ludlow, Shropshire, a collection of buildings in various styles and materials making no attempt at conformity.

After the Second World War the 1947 Town and Country Planning Act intro- duced lists of buildings that were thought worthy of preservation because of their architectural or historic interest; with this the freedom of the property owner was compromised as never before. Habituation with current planning law possibly inures us to the magnitude of this encroachment into the rights of property ownership. The implication of the Act was that an owner could no longer demolish an historic building – although in those days before the designation of conservation areas and the introduction of guidance such as PPG 15[1] preservation could be reduced to absurdity by retaining a building in an unsympathetic context.

Figure 6.2: Southgate Street, Bath, before the Second World War.

Figure 6.3: Southgate Street, Bath, Owen Luder's bland new shopping centre.

The 1960s saw a dramatic increase in commercial development in towns and cities. Private developers and local councils worked together to buy and demolish large blocks of old properties to be replaced by modern offices and shopping centres. Architects had their opportunity to introduce modern architecture to Britain on an unprecedented scale. Modernism was then the orthodox style, unchallenged by architectural criticism. Local politicians took pride in seeing out-dated buildings cleared away and replaced by the most up-to-date facilities. In Bath the City Architect and Planning Officer brushed aside criticism of Owen Luder's bland Southgate Centre with the memorable comment that the people of Bath deserved their modern shopping centres just as much as the people of Birmingham.

During the same period re-development in town and city centres was complemented by massive slum clearance programmes. Led by Public Health and Housing Officers and abetted by planners and surveyors, vast areas of traditional housing were cleared. It was by no means all slum property that was swept away; many of the houses were capable of economic rehabilitation. But they were included in housing CPO's to achieve comprehensive site clearance on a large scale, thus opening the way for architects to experiment with new forms of housing development.

Even more reprehensible than the sheer destructiveness of the period was the secrecy that surrounded development decisions. Frequently, the public had no idea what was happening in their area until the bulldozers arrived on site. Public opinion was held in contempt by architects, developers and council officials. Planning decisions were taken in private – plans were carefully locked away from public view. The attitude from the authorities was at best the paternalistic 'we know what's best for you', at worst there were elements of corruption that underlay dealings between councillors and property developers, aided by their ambitious professional advisors.

The power of public opinion

It is a truism that the public does not appreciate what it has until it is too late. The loss of familiar old streets, buildings and landmarks led to the popular protest campaigns of the 1970s. Public sentiment in favour of traditional architecture and individual ownership of property fuelled rebellion against the Modernism champ-ioned by professionals and intellectuals, and against the monopolization of land ownership by property companies and municipal authorities.

The Skeffington Report of 1969 on Public Participation in Planning along with the 1971 Town and Country Planning Act facilitated radical reforms in the planning procedure to bring the system to what we are familiar with today. The statutory requirement to notify and consult the public and amenity societies on planning appli-cations and planning proposals has undermined the cosy dialogue between property owner and the local authority.

The proliferation of residents' associ-

Figure 6.4: 'Slum clearance' in the Balance Street area of Bath.

Figure 6.5: Balance Street flats designed by Bath's City Architect.

ations, conservation area advisory committees, amenity societies such as the Georgian Group, The Victorian Society, the Twentieth Century Society and their local branch activists have brought a third force into planning. They usually take the line of defence and assemble to *prevent* things happening, such as the destruction of historic buildings and the construction of modern ones. They are consequently perceived as reactionary, particularly by the development industry and the professions that feed from it, for example the RICS and the RIBA. It is often argued that power has shifted from the pro-active relationship of landowner with local authority to a reactive one between local councillors, residents, and amenity organizations.

Who's leading whom?

Both Labour and Conservative administrations have introduced legislation and policy directives that have continued to shift power towards the conservation lobby. English Heritage, as a quasi-autonomous organization, promotes and campaigns for conservation causes with an openness denied to staff previously working within a government department.

Conservation has moved forward from a defensive, reactionary role to a proactive one. A nation-wide network of local associations and preservation trusts, supported by national organizations like the Civic Trust and the Association of Building Preservation Trusts are now formulating schemes and looking to the Heritage Lottery Fund for resources.

Architectural historians have increasingly moved from the academic world into journalism and conservation administration where they can exercise influence and power over the development process. Some who strongly favour a return to Classicism use their positions of influence to champion the likes of Quinlan Terry, Leon Krier and Robert Adam. In the 1960s and early 1970s the Bath Preservation Trust supported the case for modern architecture to take its place within the Georgian city. During the last decade the Trust has rejected this approach and is currently influencing the replacement of Owen Luder's Southgate Centre in favour of a Neo-Classical design, using their links with the Prince of Wales's Institute of Architecture.

Can it now be said that public opinion has acquired a greater say in decisions about the conservation of historic buildings and new buildings in historic towns? Maybe not, since the general public seldom gets involved except where the local media raise the profile of an issue. Those amenity organizations that claim to represent the public are usually promoting the views of a small, elite section of the community. They might be horrified if an issue were put to a local referendum! Can public taste in this country really be trusted?

Figure 6.6: Chapman Taylor & Partners 'Neo-Classical' scheme recently submitted to Bath and N E Somerset Council for planning consent.

History versus home comforts

The general public may enjoy the charming character of historic places but, when it comes to their homes, their places of work, and their routine shopping, they normally expect the very latest comforts and convenience. We generally prefer to indulge our propensity for nostalgia through TV films rather than live it out in our daily lives. Children particularly have an enthusiasm for buildings that are new and exciting, although a child's interest and concerns for historic buildings can be aroused easily – and much rewarding work is taking place in this field. But as we age, we all come to place more importance on the retention of our established surroundings for all the associations and memories they contain, and for visible links to the past that help to define our history and our place in it. So, public opinion may favour the historic street scene and its traditional architecture, whilst expecting the advantages that modern buildings bring to our daily lives.

Where do others stand? Building owners are generally unreliable guardians of our past. With numerous honourable exceptions, many private owners of historic buildings place their own monetary interests and personal convenience ahead of any public duty to preservation. Much as homeowners may profess admiration for the character of their old homes, double glazed PVC windows are irresistible when it comes to considerations of maintenance and comfort!

Public buildings and functional requirements

Historic buildings in public ownership enjoy no guaranteed security either. National Health Service administrators have very sound arguments for demolishing Victorian hospitals, as do educationalists when it comes to schools, or leisure departments responsible for historic swimming pools. Planning officers often face an unequal struggle with colleagues in property management departments within local government, and severe budgetary problems undermine even further their influence on corporate decisions affecting historic buildings. As council services diminish, business managers choose to offload the old inefficient buildings and retain the modern ones. These old buildings, which will have suffered from under-investment in maintenance over the

Figure 6.7: Birmingham Central Library, architect E M Barry, 1865, under demolition in 1971 to make way for its successor.

Figure 6.8: Birmingham Conservatoire and new Central Library, architect John Madin Design Group, completed in 1972.

years, are not perceived as supporting the council's self-image of a progressive, efficient, modern organization.

Even the Church of England and other denominations seem to place little value on the aesthetic and spiritual qualities of an historic church when seeking to provide greater warmth, comfort and social interaction for their congregations. Radical internal alterations or the abandonment of a capacious old building in favour of a compact new one may help to portray the Church as a relevant modern mission appealing to the present generation.

Commercial interest

Property developers are frequently enthusiastic about acquiring historic buildings for development projects. The distinctiveness they offer a scheme, and the public appeal of old buildings, are clear marketing advantages for the completed development. Equally, taking on problematic historic buildings wins instant support from a harassed local authority that has been pressed to serve Repairs Notices; this support can be exploited later when negotiations encounter more fundamental policy problems.

But the developer's interest in history can be superficial, and the commitment to authenticity is often weak. Perhaps worst in the field are the large breweries who strip out the genuine interiors of nineteenth-century pubs and replace them with their own image of Victoriana – or even with a style that predates the building. Developers generally are inclined to 'ham up' an historic property – adding cobbles, painted signs, and fake beams to give more 'historic impact'.

Local authority responses

So how does the local planning committee respond to property developers saving historic buildings, but seeking to make extensive alterations; to amenity societies and English Heritage demanding the highest standards of conservation and authenticity; to pressure from other council committees looking for economic development gains or seeking to promote the town as both a heritage attraction and a modern centre of business and commerce?

Committee members embrace a combination of different viewpoints. As most members have outside interests and sit on other council committees, they are likely to bring a width of perspective and influence to bear on their judgements. Often these conflicting objectives result in compromise, and façadism is a typical example. Retaining an original façade, or creating a new one in an historic style to enclose an essentially modern building, is a formula that often is advocated. Whilst many councillors are keen to encourage good modern architecture, they often lack confidence in their own judgement as to what constitutes good modern design, and are anxious not to find themselves responsible for the latest detested 'carbuncle'.

Misguided façadism?

The public reception for 'façaded' buildings generally appears favourable. They have a comfortable, familiar quality; they are not challenging; they do not disturb a familiar scene. The 'moral' questions that worry those of us who have devoted our lives to planning and architecture may not occur to people pre-occupied with other issues. Façadism apparently provides the ideal compromise for many people, combining a modern functional interior within an established recognizable exterior. It is the formula that speculative house builders have relied upon for years.

Research carried out by Dr Phil Hubbard[2] has demonstrated the differing preferences between building professionals and the general public, the public being predominantly predisposed towards buildings that incorporate traditional elements, and may be defined as 'historicist'. Hubbard writes:

> This appeared not to be because of their perceived beauty per se, but because of the contribution that such traditional architectural reference made to people's sense of stability and identity. This indicates that people appreciate a sense of continuity in the townscape and that a violent disruption of the built environment can be antithetical to the wishes of the populace. Attachment to buildings and places results when the lifestyles symbolized by a place are congruent with traditional community values with which people can identify.

He goes on to identify the design features that the public are most concerned about, 'the pattern of fenestration, contextual compatibility, design details and façade openness' (rather than the siting, massing, scale and size, which are generally deemed to be matters that properly fall within the ambit of development control.)

How, then, are the views of the public at large communicated to planners, and how are those views carried into the planning mechanisms and ultimately into the building? The planning system regularly and systematically facilitates public comment on a project by project basis. Less frequent opportunities are available for the public to contribute to local action plans for wider policy formulation. The

Figures 6.9 and 6.10: The Colonnades, Bath, a 1980s three-level shopping centre built behind the eighteenth-century, Grade I listed façade to Bath Street.

general public are more disposed to participate in discussions about specific projects that affect them directly, than to engage in more abstract debate about long-term policies. To that extent, any public consultation on general strategies covering urban design or development guidelines is unlikely to draw a significant public response. It is, however, at this stage that any planning policy generally affecting design should be established as the basis for specific planning decisions.

At the level of the detailed planning application, when more public interest is generated, the local authority planning officers will guide the committee members to assess the project against any policy background established at a generic level. Officers are likely to discourage members from becoming closely involved in matters of architectural style, irrespective of public opinion. To that extent, any public preference for an historicist approach to design is unlikely to influence decisions explicitly through the formal planning machinery.

Of course, planning officers themselves may have encouraged an historicist approach to design in pre-application discussions with the applicant and architect. They are likely to do this if it fits with their own preference, or if they are conscious of a similar strong preference on the part of a majority or a persuasive minority of members on the planning committee.

In this way developers and their architects may elect to opt for an historicist approach to design in the expectation (whether or not it is intimated by the officers) that this will lead to a quicker and favourable planning decision. In so far that councillors may personally share the views of the public, or may choose to reflect those views in the interests of democratic accountability (or electoral popularity), then a public preference for historicism may influence the design approach for a proportion of development in this country. It is, therefore, more likely to happen through an osmotic process rather than through the formal machinery of public consultation and participation.

Where does this all lead to with regard to the quality of our historic cities? It certainly points towards modern functional interiors masked by newly-built, historicist, traditional street frontages or preserved façades. We are left with new buildings pretending to be old, and genuine old buildings looking ridiculously new. The artist and musician use the technology of their age and are expected to challenge conventional taste – whilst doing so with an understanding of tradition and context. The architect's role should not be so different.

Figure 6.11: The 1976 extension to the Birmingham School of Jewellery in the Jewellery Quarter Conservation Area.

Conclusion

If our historic cities are to be more than Disneyland stage sets for the tourist industry, they must accommodate modern buildings meeting current-day requirements. Our architects must produce buildings that are recognizable of our own age but with an understanding and respect for history and context. If this involves some challenges to public taste and convention, it may not be a bad thing. At the same time we should treat our historic buildings with care and integrity, minimizing the changes they undergo to meet current needs, and maximizing their authenticity. Then we may achieve a situation where our historic towns continue to embrace buildings of different periods and styles (including our own) without upsetting their essential characteristics; where new is distinguishable from old, and where debate and controversy ensure that professional scrutiny and public interest are alive and well.

References

1. DEPARTMENT OF THE ENVIRONMENT & DEPARTMENT OF NATIONAL HERITAGE: *PPG15 Planning Policy Guidance: Planning the and Historic Environment*, HMSO, 1994.

2. HUBBARD, P J, *Attitudes to Redevelopment in Birmingham's City Centre: An Examination of Architectural Interpretation*, Cheltenham and Gloucester College of Higher Education, February, 1994.

The planner's perspective: a view from the front

Mansell Jagger Director of Planning, Canterbury City Council

Summary

A great deal of damage was caused to the fabric of many historic cities through bombing during the Second World War and in its aftermath by all too enthusiastic planners and developers who were, often misguidedly, trying to create new environments for the post-war society. Canterbury was one of those cities that suffered insensitive development during the 1950s and 1960s.

In this chapter, Mansell Jagger, who has been Director of Planning in Canterbury since 1986, describes how during the past twenty years there has been a major shift in philosophy towards development in the city, which extends to 'repairing the historic townscape'. The medieval and Georgian buildings have been carefully conserved, and some of the large 1950s and 1960s developments have been completely redeveloped on a smaller scale based on vernacular styles, using traditional materials. However, he warns of the dangers of not doing it with due attention to detail.

By his own admission, this is a controversial approach but as he points out it is very popular with the local community. He defends his position, along with other planning authorities at the front line in the battle to preserve the historic environment, as a duty to act in the public rather than the private interest. He throws up a challenge to architectural schools and practices to develop on regional and local traditions and concludes by describing the brief for the next phase of redevelopment in Canterbury that calls for '.... essentially a new district .... providing a unique opportunity for a sympathetic late twentieth-century addition to the historic city in contemporary style.'

Introduction

When the past feeds and sustains the present and future you have a civilized society. It was only in this century that we broke with the past .... we should build cities, towns and villages which seem to have grown out of the historical fabric of Britain. *HRH The Prince of Wales*[1]

In his book *A Vision of Britain*, the Prince of Wales made the fundamental point that you cannot attempt to plan or design for the future without a sound understanding of the past. He made a strong plea for continuity in planning and building, and for what we now call 'contextual design'. Visit any historic town in this country and you will see the damage caused in the post-war years by architects, planners and engineers who had little understanding of, and even less sympathy for, the history and development of the place where they were working. However, all is not lost; in recent years there have been welcome signs that professionals have learned from past mistakes and that there has been a fundamental shift in the philosophy of how we should plan and design in historic areas.

Public opinion and official guidance

It was not the professionals who stopped the municipal vandalism of the 1950s and 1960s but public opinion. Through the Civic Trust, the *Civic Amenities Act* came onto the statute book in 1967,

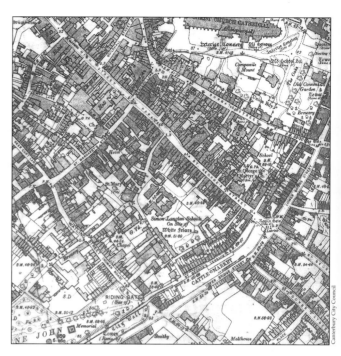

Figure 7.1: *Plan of pre-war Canterbury.*

Figure 7.2: *Aerial photograph of Canterbury showing post-war development.*

introducing 'conservation areas' for the protection, not just of individual buildings, but of whole areas of architectural and historic interest. Public concern about new development has increased steadily until it is now in constant focus. In response, the government has given local planning authorities powers to control change in conservation areas and has encouraged them to prepare design briefs for particular sites and design guidance for their town or district. Several authorities have published design guides: for example, the *North Norfolk Design Guide*[2] gives sensible and straightforward guidance on what to do in that area. Others, like Canterbury, have included design guidance in their local plans.[3]

Where design guidance has been the subject of public consultation prior to adoption by the local planning authority, one can expect it to be backed by planning inspectors on appeal and planning officers will expect architects and developers to have read the guidance before submitting planning applications. It seems that the number of architects who approach the design of a new building 'cold', without some research into the history and context of the site, appears to be diminishing. The quality of design in historic areas also seems to have improved dramatically in recent years, which is a product of more informed dialogue between architects and planners and an increasing appreciation of the value of a contextual and, perhaps, 'populist' approach to design.

For far too long, professional egotism and self-interest produced buildings that, though appreciated perhaps by the cognoscenti, are disliked by the general public. Concluding a television interview a few years ago, the eminent architect Terry Farrell remarked 'What is wrong with designing buildings that people actually like?' A good question! Some architects say that the problem arises because the public does not understand their designs and needs educating to appreciate modern buildings. It seems, however, that if people dislike what is designed and do not understand what the architect is trying to achieve, then at least some fault and need for education lies with the designer. The Prince of Wales put it rather well in his Principles of Architecture: 'Let the people who will have to live with what you build help guide your hand.'[4]

In the Department of the Environment's 1994 report *Quality in Town & Country*, the then Secretary of State, the Rt Hon John Gummer MP, was very keen to promote the protection of the built heritage and the improvement of the quality of new design. One of the key questions he raised was how to achieve new design that would both enhance local character and reinforce a sense of community.[5] In my view the answer is by designing in context.

I make no apologies for what may be described as a populist approach. Town planners like myself, and the local planning authorities for which we work, are at the front-line in the battle to preserve our historic towns and villages. Planners and planning authorities have had to be responsive to public opinion for many years now, since their duty, enshrined in the planning system of this country, is to act in the public rather than the private interest. The position of the architect is often quite

different. Architects usually work for clients whose interest seldom extends beyond
their own site. In the 1990 annual report of Royal Fine Art Commission, Chairman,
Lord St John of Fawsley, said, 'The architect is not like a painter, exercising a
sacrosanct artistic birthright to put on canvas whatever, for the moment, grabs his
psyche. He is operating in the public realm and it is necessary and right that the
community as represented by the local planning authority should set limits on, and
point the direction for, what he does.'[6]

So how do architects go about designing new buildings that will fit into historic
settings? Most importantly they must understand the place, its history and how it
has developed over the centuries. Only then can they think about managing the
continuity with the past whilst developing for the future. The local design guidance
should be used, which should be about identifying and building on local character
and a sense of place. Essentially, a design philosophy needs to be agreed.
Canterbury is a useful example of a city to show the evolution of a philosophy and
the impact that it has had on the design of new buildings in historic settings.

The Canterbury example

Canterbury has been developing a contextual – some would say historicist –
approach to new design for almost twenty years. To understand the philosophy
adopted in Canterbury, firstly the background must be understood. The need for a
new approach arose out of the loss through bombing during the Second World War
of a significant part of the historic city, followed by over twenty years of further
destruction of the historic fabric by the then city council through comprehensive
redevelopment and highway schemes.

The citizens believed, not without some justification, that the city council was
intent on destroying the old city and rebuilding it on the lines of a 1960s New Town.
When Lewis Braithwaite surveyed the local planning scene for the *Architectural
Review* in 1967, he was horrified. 'Canterbury is not yet ruined' he wrote, 'but it
soon will be if the City Plan, which proposes the destruction of much of what
remains, is implemented.'[7]

When the new city council came into being in 1974, there was a fundamental
change of approach: a realization that the destruction had to stop and that the fabric
of the city needed to be repaired; that there should be an end to the construction of
flat roofed concrete boxes in the 'anywhere' style of modern architecture; and a
need to adopt a new conservation-led philosophy before the historic city was
destroyed for ever.

In the last twenty years Canterbury has successfully pulled itself out of the mire
and is becoming again the vibrant, attractive and lived-in small city it once was.
Most of the traffic has been removed from within the city walls: the marvellous
collection of medieval and Georgian buildings has been restored with grant-aid in

Figures 7.3 & 7.4: Longmarket, Butchery Lane – before and after redevelopment (below). Architects: Robert Semple of Building Design Partnership (Belfast) with Anthony Swaine (Canterbury).

partnership with property owners, and many of the sites that had been cleared since the war have now been redeveloped with new buildings in traditional styles and materials.

During the last ten years the economic prosperity of the city has seen opportunities arising to redevelop some of those sites that were themselves redeveloped in the 1950s and 1960s following wartime bombing. The Longmarket is a particularly good example of a very popular development where two ancient streets, Burgate and Butchery Lane, have been rebuilt in traditional fashion.

The city council's approach is now based on three fundamental concepts – Conservation, Continuity and Context.

Conservation

There is no point in designating an area for its special interest and then allowing its character to be damaged by destroying buildings or other features that make it special, or by allowing new development that is out of place, scale or context with the area. Architects need to have a real understanding of what constitutes the special architectural and historic interest of the area and be aware of the basic test that will be applied to any planning application, which is that any development must preserve or enhance the special character and appearance of the area.

Continuity

Our towns and villages have individual, unique identities, derived in many cases from hundreds of years of slow change and development. In most, the historic form of development is still visible. If the historic street pattern is altered or the ancient plot boundaries obliterated, the historic interest of a town or village is destroyed just as surely as if its historic buildings are demolished.

In one quarter of the historic centre of Canterbury, the continuity of a thousand years was destroyed by post-war replanning that ignored the context of history; this is mirrored in so many of our historic towns and cities. This understanding of the need for continuity has only recently been acknowledged by many professionals in this country, though the public have recognized it for some time. It is interesting to compare the different views of heritage after the Second World War in other European countries that have suffered more destruction than the United Kingdom. Compare the rebuilding of cities like Warsaw, Leningrad or St Malo, where there appears to have been a real feeling of loss, of wanting to regain a cultural identity by repair and reconstruction, not by simply erasing the past.

To see the principles of continuity and tradition applied at their best, visit Ypres in Belgium where a superb medieval town has been lovingly and meticulously reconstructed over a period of seventy-five years following its complete destruction in the First World War.

The reconstruction of towns like Ypres, Arras (France, *see Figure 4.1*), or Tournai (Belgium) provides an object lesson for architects and planners working in war damaged towns like Dubrovnik and Zadar in Croatia and elsewhere, and should inform us in this country how to tackle redevelopment in our historic towns.

Figures 7.5 & 7.6 Longmarket, Burgate – before and after (below) redevelopment. Architects: Robert Semple of Building Design Partnership (Belfast) with Anthony Swaine (Canterbury).

Canterbury has adopted a philosophy of repair for the damaged fabric of the city, which is not just repairing and restoring historic buildings, but it extends to repairing the historic townscape – for example filling gaps in streets caused by wartime bombing or post-war clearance, or where there is an opportunity to replace poor quality modern buildings with traditionally designed buildings that fit the historic street and plot boundaries.

Historical research is encouraged in order to establish the context of the proposal and to understand the continuity of development that will guide the new construction on the site. There is a great deal known about the development of Canterbury over the centuries from both archaeological excavations and detailed surveys of historic buildings. All new developments are preceded by archaeological investigations, usually by the Canterbury Archaeological Trust, which offers its expertise and knowledge on the history of any site, whilst the City Planning Department has extensive map and photographic collections that can be consulted.

Context

Since the test for new development is whether it preserves or enhances the special character or appearance of the conservation area, it follows that new buildings will usually be expected to fit in with their surroundings.

English Heritage has produced some useful guidelines:

> In considering proposals for new buildings in conservation areas the principal concerns should be the appropriateness of the overall mass or volume of the building, its scale, ... and its relationship with its context –whether it sits comfortably. The new building should be in harmony with, or complementary to, its neighbours, having regard to the adjoining architectural styles. The use of materials generally matching those which are historically dominant in the area is important, as is the need for the development not to have a visually disruptive impact on the existing townscape or street scene. It should also, as far as possible, fit into the 'grain' of an historic area, for example by respecting surviving medieval street patterns. All these aspects can be assessed to a large degree without reference to the architectural style adopted for the design, whether contemporary or historicist.[8]

Figure 7.7: St Peter's Lane. Berkeley Homes (Kent) Ltd. Architects: OSEL Architects (Surrey).

These are excellent principles but they will not guarantee good design or beautiful buildings: architects dislike discussing style, preferring to refer to something called 'good modern architecture', but the question of style cannot be dismissed so easily.

The last fifty years have seen the rise and fall of Modernism in Britain. But, if Modernism has had its day, what is to replace it and what kind of architecture should take its place in historic areas? In the last few years we have had a plethora of 'architectural-isms': Post-Modernism, Neo-Classicism, Post-Functionalism and so on. On the other hand, some architects

Figure 7.8: Broad Street. Left: The Bowers. Townscape Designs Ltd. Architects: Cattell Skinner Design Partnership (Canterbury). Right: Malvern House, The King's School. Architects: Lee Evans de Moubray (Canterbury).

still seem to want to try and discover a new single universal style for the late twentieth century –'a reflection of contemporary society'. But we live in an increasingly pluralistic society. 'Pluralist societies .... naturally develop a plurality of culture, and thus, eventually, eclecticism of style. Hence the architectural eclecticism of our late twentieth-century western world.'[9]

This does not mean that anything goes! It means that there is no *one* accepted style to hang your design hat on. At the 1990 *Civilising the City* conference, Edinburgh architect James Simpson deplored the absence of 'morality of style' in contemporary architecture and pleaded for an end to 'designer architecture.'[10] He deplored the fact that most architects lacked the training in traditional and conservation skills, which are essential for working in historic areas. Simpson had a good point. It is not so many years ago that a graduate from one of our architectural schools pointed out that a basic tenet of the teaching was that 'if it doesn't have a flat roof it can't be modern architecture.'

It is the character of the place that should be reflected in contextual design. Since one place is different from the next, it is vital that the designer understands the local character. For example, apart from the Cathedral and a handful of other buildings, the historic city of Canterbury is largely made up of modest domestic scale, vernacular buildings, craftsman-builder rather than architect designed, and this is equally true of many of Britain's smaller historic towns.

You know you are in Canterbury, not just because you glimpse the Cathedral towers over the rooftops, but because the amalgam of building styles, forms, materials and details is unique to Canterbury, and that is also true elsewhere. The question is how do you capture the spirit, the character of the place, in new design?

One way, of course, is to reconstruct. In some circumstances it may be acceptable to copy what was there before, even though there might be a considerable gap between the destruction of the old and the building of the new. Ernst Schirmacher's 1983 reconstruction of stone and timber-framed buildings in Römemberg Square, Frankfurt replacing houses destroyed by bombing in 1944, caused considerable controversy when first put forward in a competition. 'The architectural jury, sticking to its Modernist tenets, argued vehemently against them but were ignored by the mayor and town council, who insisted the scheme be built. Long before it was completed, the architectural press subjected the scheme to universal vilification, only to find that it was broadly welcomed in Frankfurt.'[11]

Another way, becoming more popular, is to design in traditional styles. One of the delights of travelling in other countries is to see traditional design and buildings techniques still being employed, particularly in small towns and villages, maintaining the continuity of interest that I believe to be so vital. Switzerland is a good example where you will see traditional chalets still being constructed, or New England where traditional clapboard houses are still the mainstay of the housing market, though the designs may change in style and detail over the years.

Local tradition is important, and its importance to local people has grown proportionately to the destruction of local traditions and heritage in the post-war years. Public taste tends to be conservative – there is nothing wrong with that – and 'modern architecture' has become associated with mass, high-rise public housing and Brutalist town centre redevelopments.

House builders, at least, understand that people want period character without the problems of owning old buildings. 'Replica Georgian, Edwardian or Victorian designs may be derided by the purists, but they are popular with the buyers' reported *The Sunday Telegraph*, which quotes the new houses being built by Berkeley Homes in the redevelopment of the area around Canterbury West Station.[12] For twenty years Canterbury has encouraged architects to

Figure 7.9: Northgate, Lanfranc House (Christchurch College). Architects: Pentangle Design Group (Herts)

Shirley Binyon, Canterbury City Council

design in traditional style, particularly in filling gaps in streets. This is sometimes ridiculed, ignorantly I think, as 'pastiche' but if done properly it can, I believe, take its valid place alongside other more 'contemporary' approaches. However, a word of warning: our experience is that if this approach is to be successful then it has to be done properly – down to the last detail. It is no use stopping short: a building in the Georgian style will look silly if there are no glazing bars to the windows, or if there are features or details from other periods mixed in. In other words, the design must be informed. One of the problems encountered, even in Canterbury, is the limited number of architects with real knowledge and experience of such matters.

Architects brought up in the ethos of the Modern Movement tend to feel uneasy at the idea of designing in traditional styles, preferring the approach commonly propounded by architects and planners alike: 'to design in modern style but in sympathy with the historic character of the area' – something that is far more easily said than done.

In the 1960s and 1970s it was often thought enough to add some brick or tile cladding to the structural box to make it fit with its surroundings. During 1980s there was a re-emergence of the pitched tile or slated roof; using local materials and traditional roof forms is particularly important in small towns and villages where the whole settlement is seen in its landscape setting, or where views are obtained over the rooftops from vantage points.

Using local materials will help, but is not the whole answer. So often, it seems that traditional forms, features and details are reduced to a series of motifs applied in a way that seeks to be new and fresh but frequently looks contrived and quickly dates; the buildings then tend to suffer from comparison with their historic neighbours because they lack decoration and detailing.

Figure 7.10: Station Road West. Berkeley Homes (Kent) Ltd. Architects: Clyde Design Partnership (Canterbury).

Figure 7.11: Barton Mill Court. McCarthy & Stone. Architects: Philip Johnson (The Planning Bureau).

The real challenge is: how do you design something that is modern and yet fits in and is obviously of that place? In particular, how do you design buildings that are of a greater scale than those built in past centuries but still sit happily in the context of the place? It would be nice to think that architectural schools and practices might take up the challenge of developing on regional and local traditions to take us into the new millennium with contemporary architecture set firmly within its historic context and displaying that essential continuity with the past.

Conclusion

We have thrown down a big challenge in Canterbury. In the next few years nearly twelve acres of the Whitefriars area inside the city walls will be redeveloped. This was an area that was developed following extensive bombing during the last war and includes some very large buildings including a department store and multi-storey car park. Some of the buildings are only twenty years old. Everyone is mightily sick of the sight of them.

Here the changes in the use of land and buildings and in the basic layout of the area in the post-war years were so fundamental that it is not possible to contemplate the restoration of the pre-war pattern of streets and buildings. The Brief calls for: 'The construction of what is essentially a new district within the walls providing a unique opportunity for a sympathetic late twentieth-century addition to the historic city in contemporary style. The architectural challenge will be to design buildings, streets and squares on a scale and pattern which will fit with the grain of the historic city and which will not only contribute to, but become a permanent part of the special character of Canterbury.'[13] To paraphrase the Prince of Wales, the new development should 'seem to have grown out of the historical fabric' of Canterbury.

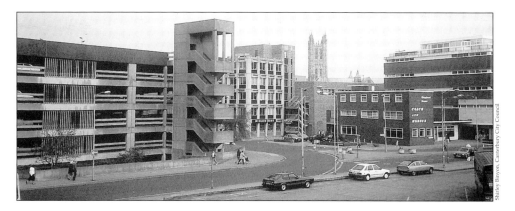

Figure 7.12: Whitefriars, Canterbury.

This is a very significant move away from the indoor shopping centre mentality of recent years and a reversion to the values of traditional urban and civic design. The lessons to be learned from the Longmarket, Whitefriars and other recent buildings in Canterbury will, I believe, be invaluable to all of us who hold dear to our hearts the conservation and future success of our priceless historic towns.

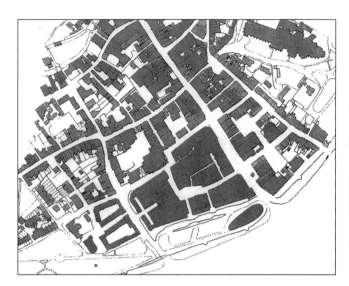

Figure 7.13: Plan of Canterbury showing the 'grain' of the proposed Whitefriars development (lower centre) in relation to the historic city.

References

1 WALES, HRH The Prince of, *A Vision of Britain* Doubleday 1989.
2 NORTH NORFOLK COUNTY COUNCIL, *North Norfolk Design Guide,* 1989 (now included in District Local Plan 1995).
3 CANTERBURY CITY COUNCIL, *Canterbury District Local Plan* – Deposit Draft, 1994.
4 WALES, HRH The Prince of, *op.cit.*
5 DEPARTMENT OF THE ENVIRONMENT, *Quality in Town & Country,* 1994.
6 ROYAL FINE ART COMMISSION, *28th Annual Report 1990,* HMSO, 1991.
7 BRAITHWAITE, Lewis, 'Canterbury: historic town or write-off?' *The Architectural Review,* October 1967.
8 ENGLISH HERITAGE, *Conservation Area Practice,* 1993.
9 CROOK, J Mordaunt, *The Dilemma of Style: Architectural Ideas from the Picturesque to the Post Modern,* John Murray, 1989.
10 SIMPSON, James, 'Whither Conservation?' Proceedings from the conference *Civilising the City: Quality or Chaos in Historic Towns,* Nic Allen Publishing, Edinburgh, 1990.
11 WORSLEY, Giles, 'Sure to offend' *Country Life,* 8 October 1992.
12 RUSSELL, Rosalind, 'Out with the old' *The Sunday Telegraph,* 12 February 1997.
13 CANTERBURY CITY COUNCIL, *The Whitefriars, Canterbury – Development Brief,* June 1996.

Assessing quality:
the pertinent criteria for designing buildings in historic settings

Sherban Cantacuzino *Former Secretary of the Royal Fine Art Commission*

Summary

From 1979 to 1994 Sherban Cantacuzino was Secretary of the Royal Fine Art Commission, the London-based advisory body that is consulted on the design of the most important and prominently sited projects in England and Wales. In 1994 his book What makes a Good Building? *was published, which was the result of an inquiry commissioned by then Secretary of State for Heritage, Peter Brooke. In this chapter Sherban Cantacuzino takes his criteria for a good building a stage further and relates them to placing new buildings in historic settings.*

He begins and ends with the need for 'beauty' in architecture, which he believes is the essential criterion. Within this there are other requirements including the truthful expression of the function of a building; an integrity or honesty of construction, as illustrated for example in the true principles of Gothic or Classical architecture; a simplicity of design, which displays no superfluous parts and exactly answers its ends; and harmony, which is required both within the building and in its relationship to the wider urban environment.

Unlike Mansell Jagger in the previous chapter, who from a planner's perspective champions a return to vernacular styles and the use of traditional materials, Sherban Cantacuzino advocates the preservation of scale, texture and harmony rather than a return to original styles or unmistakably modern designs. In the end he concludes that what really makes a good building is enlightened architectural patronage.

Introduction

I am going to jump in at the deep end and begin by discussing beauty. It is unfashionable to speak about beauty because it is an absolute value; few people nowadays are prepared to accept that there are such things as absolute values that are permanent. What is beautiful is not just a transitory matter of personal opinion; beauty is not just in the eye of the beholder. There has been a wide consensus for a considerable period of time that the dome of St Peter's in Rome is beautiful. As an individual you need not like it, but you cannot go against the verdict of time and consensus and deny that it is beautiful. You may like something because it is fashionable but as a judge you have to distinguish between what you like and what you recognize as 'good'.

Beauty has been associated most readily with truth and simplicity. In his writings John Keats tells us that he 'never can feel certain of any truth but from a clear perception of beauty.'[1] He speaks of 'the truth of imagination – what imagination seizes as beauty must be truth.'[2] And, more simply, in *Ode on a Grecian Urn*, he says 'Beauty is truth, truth beauty, that is all/Ye know on earth, and all ye need to know.'[3]

The view that something has to be simple to be beautiful is unfashionable and has been ever since Robert Venturi first published his influential book, *Complexity and Contradiction in Architecture*.[4] Yet the best definition of beauty that I know is Emerson's, and is related to simplicity: 'We ascribe beauty to that which is simple; which has no superfluous parts; which exactly answers its end.'[5] The Abbé Laugier in his exhortation *Soyez simple et naturel*[6] combined simplicity with truth, for 'natural' means 'open', 'honest', 'truthful'. It is interesting to note that Philip Larkin, when he was chairman of the Booker Prize judges in 1977, dealt with exactly the same points when he asked of the novels he was considering: 'First, could I read it? If I could read it, did I believe it? If I believed it, did I care about it?'and finally, 'Would I go on caring about it?'[7] Simplicity and intelligibility (can I read it?), truth (can I believe it?), and fashion versus timeless qualities (do I care about it and would I go on caring about it?), the same questions can be applied to architecture.

Truth

Truth has many aspects. There is, first of all, *expression* – the apt or truthful expression of the function of a building, which enables us to recognize a building for what it is. Palladio's churches in Venice are examples of façades that express the plan and section of the building. The principal space of the tall nave and the subsidiary lower spaces of the aisles are expressed on the west front of these churches by a major central temple-front flanked by two half temple-fronts. The interpenetration of the temple-fronts produces an effect of great unity, reflecting the

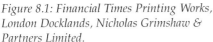

Figure 8.1: Financial Times Printing Works, London Docklands, Nicholas Grimshaw & Partners Limited.

Figure 8.2: Marco Polo Building, Battersea, London, I D Pollard.

spatial unity of the interior. These west fronts not only address the lagoon or the *campo* in an appropriate manner but, in their unity, are a symbol of the indivisible church both in a physical and spiritual sense.

Just as a temple-front may be considered an apt representation of a church or a court of law, so the transparent wall revealing the printing presses in *The Financial Times* building in London Docklands by Nicholas Grimshaw & Partners *(Figure 8.1)* could be considered an apt representation of a free and open press – of free speech in effect. The grand porticoes of Ian Pollard's Marco Polo building in Battersea, on the other hand, monumentalize the mundane activity of office work and are a grotesque misrepresentation *(Figure 8.2)*. We might consider the oriels of Michael Hopkins's Bracken House in the City of London a more appropriate and true representation of an office function *(see Figure 8.10)*.

Integrity

Another aspect of truth is *integrity* or *honesty* – the result of a strict adherence to principles of design, not in the sense of rules that may determine the design of a Classical façade, but in the sense that Gothic architecture embodies principles of construction that are quite different from the principles of Classical architecture. In

Figure 8.3: Senior Combination Room, Downing College, Cambridge, Howell, Killick, Partridge & Amis.

Gothic architecture a masonry form of frame and panel construction was invented, the frame being the buttress and the panel the windows between. The Gothic pointed arch made possible the clerestory, the flying buttress and a great deal more light inside the building. Of historical structural forms only the Gothic pointed arch is self-supporting.

Gothic principles are very clearly demonstrated in the Senior Combination Room at Downing College, Cambridge *(Figure 8.3)*. Designed some twenty-five years ago by W G Howell of Howell, Killick, Partridge & Amis, it is a small building of great integrity. The context is William Wilkins's Greek Revival buildings, which are almost free-standing and set in a landscape of lawns and trees. Respecting this strong three-dimensional quality, Howell placed his square, pavilion-like building in the same relationship with a monumental stone wall as Wilkins's temple-like college dining hall, that is in front of, and all but detached from, the wall that runs behind linking the two buildings and also screening the messy kitchen quarters on the other side. The challenge of Wilkins's porticoes demanded monumentality; the architect achieved this by expressing the structure both on the outside and on the inside of the building. The bold proportions and the vestigial Classical form of the structure – the four broken pediments are a logical expression of the folded roofslab – give this little building the grandeur that it needs to fulfil its ceremonial function.

If Gothic architecture embodies the principles of separation and articulation of the separate parts, modern

Figure 8.4: Office buildings, Bedfont Lakes, Middlesex, Michael Hopkins and Partners.

building methods have made these principles manifest in construction and assembly. In Michael Hopkins's little known office buildings at Bedfont Lakes near Heathrow *(Figure 8.4)*, the frame-and-panel construction is clearly and consistently expressed, the size of stanchion diminishes as it rises and has less load to carry. In his design of the new parliamentary building opposite the Houses of Parliament in London *(Figures 8.5 & 8.6)*, the complexity of ducts rising alongside the piers and continuing visibly up the slope of the roof is an accompaniment to the frame-and-panel construction of stone piers and bronze windows. Like the stanchions at Bedfont Lakes, the solid load-bearing piers decrease in cross-sectional area as the load lightens on their upward journey, while on either side vertical bronze ducts increase in cross-sectional area as they gather more air on their way up.

Making a building 'legible' and intelligible in this way is part of the quest for truth, which enables us to say 'I can read it and I can believe it.' But we cannot make a fair judgement of a building without knowing a good deal more about the building than merely its external appearance. We need to know the building's function, the way the building responds to specific needs like energy efficiency, the way the building is constructed, the materials with which it is built and the way it fits into the overall plan of the area. Design covers not only the façade, but also the plan and section of the building. A façade must not only address the street or square in front of it, but must also bear some relation to the plan and section that lie behind it. A façade that conceals the truth, or sets out to deceive, is clearly an obstacle to comprehension and appreciation.

Figures 8.5 & 8.6: Project for the new Parliamentary Building, Westminster, London, Michael Hopkins and Partners; view from the river and detail of the façade

Quinlan Terry's Neo-Georgian riverside development at Richmond *(Figure 8.7)* has façades that deny the plan and section. What we see is not a number of separate buildings, but one or two large office buildings with open office floors extending across what we might be forgiven for assuming to be party walls. Quinlan Terry imitates Georgian so convincingly that it is no longer possible to tell which part is new. Compelling economic reasons make traditional architecture of this kind, which is based on solid load-bearing wall construction, virtually impossible unless we are prepared to dress up and conceal the steel or concrete frame – pretend, in other words, that the construction is of solid load-bearing walls.

Before leaving the search for truth in design, I would like to discuss detail and ornament: detail in modern architecture fulfilling a similar role to ornament or decoration in traditional architecture. The question is whether the detail or ornament is intrinsic or merely added. Architects who make use of the Classical language in their architecture have an advantage because the rules have been there for centuries. Even if the Classical decoration of the Richmond riverside development is not much more than a veneer both inside and out, it is pleasing to the eye and, especially inside, gives the spaces a sense of order and scale often lacking in modern rooms.

In modern buildings there is often an absence of detail. The buildings of *The Economist* group in London *(Figures 8.8 & 8.9)*, by Alison and Peter Smithson, a classic of 30 years ago, consist of a simple frame-and-panel construction (so simple, in fact, that the late Theo Crosby called it 'baby talk') with the detail limited to the joints of panel to frame and panel to panel, and to the attenuation of the frame itself, which (once again) reduces in cross-section as it rises up the building and carries progressively less load. In the façade of the Marco Polo building *(Figure 8.2)* there is

Figure 8.7: Riverside development at Richmond, Surrey, Quinlan Terry.

Figures 8.8 & 8.9: The Economist group of buildings, St James's Street, London, Alison and Peter Smithson.

virtually no detail at all, the alternating surfaces of shiny white re-crystallized glass and black window glass being almost totally devoid of modelling or articulation.

Lack of detail impoverishes architecture and deprives us of a layer of experience that brings us into close contact with a building where we can admire the beauty of materials and the skill of the craftsman or engineer. *The Financial Times* building embodies not only the principle of separating structure from infill but also the principle of showing how the building is put together by articulating the spidery structure that supports the glass wall.

Simplicity

Turning now to another quality that pertains to beauty, the quality of simplicity. Emerson's definition, 'we ascribe beauty to that which is simple; which has no superfluous parts; which exactly answers its end', goes well beyond mere simplicity, to order, unity, coherence, balance, harmony. The creative energy of the architect as artist has always been associated with the search for, and the making of order, manifest in architecture through symmetry, balance, and repetition. The grid, the bay, the frame – what Colin Rowe, in identifying one of the major themes of twentieth-century architecture, has called, 'the frame as a symbol of order.'[8] The satisfying quality of indivisible unity, which all the best architecture possesses, is a consequence of this search for order. It would be hard to imagine a better use of the frame to create order and unity than in *The Economist* group of buildings, between which there is a strong family likeness: they all have a reinforced concrete column structure, which is expressed on the outside and faced with Portland roach; but the spacing of the columns of the residential building is half the width, expressing its domestic function by adopting a domestic scale. In plan all the buildings have chamfered corners, which reduce the apparent bulk and open the possibility of cross-views between them. Strict adherence to design principles and economy of materials gives this scheme great coherence and integrity.

The astonishing thing about the new Bracken House in the City of London *(Figure 8.10)* is that the architect, Michael Hopkins, has achieved an extraordinary degree of unity despite having had to retain, restore and integrate the two wings of the old Bracken House by Albert Richardson – two wings, incidentally, which were not even alike. Where Richardson had set the central part of the building back, Hopkins brought it forward in a bold convex curve, serrated into a continuous row of oriels. The curve helps to reconcile the differences in the two wings and produces deeply recessed junctions that articulate the different parts of the building. Where Richardson had entrances in the wings, Hopkins gives the building a new orientation by putting the only front entrance in the middle of the new central part where there is no mistaking it, its curved canopy of opaque glass and its double-storey height breaking into the oriels above and anticipating the full-height top-lit atrium, which can be glimpsed from the street.

The division of Richardson's wings into base, middle, cornice and attic storey is carried through in the new central block; and the 'weight' of the attic storey – the ratio of the solid to void – is much the same in both. Otherwise, the central block, with its light-reflecting glass walls and recessed base, stands in some contrast to the more solid, light-absorbent surfaces and projecting base of Richardson's wings. But the fact that the oriels are serrated in plan and load-bearing gives them a degree of solidity and visual strength, which reduces the contrast and helps them to harmonize with the masonry,

Figure 8.10: Bracken House, City of London, Michael Hopkins and Partners.

bronze and cast-iron construction of Richardson. It is important to understand that the curved wall of oriels is much more than skin-deep. It relates directly to the peristyle of columns that follows the same curve behind the oriels and is part of a radial structure of beams spanning back to the curved piers at the four corners of the central core. We can say confidently of Bracken House that it has no superfluous parts and that it exactly answers its end.

Harmony

Creating harmony is largely a matter of relationships. The different parts of Bracken House, old and new, have undoubtedly been brought together into a harmonious whole by one creative mastermind. But there is also the harmony of the wider urban environment. A building may be harmonious in itself and in harmony with its neighbours. It may also be in contrast with its neighbours, and there are, of course, many degrees of contrast. In so far as contrast may result in discord and disunity we can say that, in the quest for beauty, it is better to aim for harmony and to avoid too much contrast. According to Stravinsky 'Contrast is an element of variety, but it divides our attention. Similarity is born out of a striving for unity.'[9] The consistency, regularity, formality of a street or square, or the homogeneity of an area are best respected in any new work; and to be able to show this respect it is necessary first to recognize, analyse and understand the qualities of the place.

There is the need then for critical appreciation and knowledge of existing buildings, and it is essential to get these basics right, for example height, massing and silhouette, before considering elevational treatment. The most appropriate and harmonious designs are often quite ordinary, like Leonard Manasseh's Crown Court building at King's Lynn *(Figure 8.11)*, or the beautifully restrained Theological Faculty Library of Louvain University in Belgium by Paul van Aerschot

Figure 8.11: Crown Court, King's Lynn (centre), Leonard Manasseh Partnership.

(Figure 8.12). It is a matter, primarily, of whether the new work preserves the scale of the setting and whether its colour and texture and general outline harmonize with its surroundings. A good solution is far more likely to be reached by an architect who has these points firmly in mind rather than one who starts from the assumption that all will be well if either the building is designed in its original style or if it is designed in an unmistakably modern manner. What I am saying is not support for anodyne contextualism but criticism of the architect who designs from outside inwards, deciding on the style of a building before considering function and purpose, structure and materials, and the appropriate use of technology.

Figure 8.12: Library of Theology Faculty, University of Louvain, Belgium, Paul van Aerschot.

If, as I said at the beginning, beauty is not just in the eye of the beholder but a matter of consensus and an absolute value, beauty is nevertheless 'bought', as Shakespeare observed, 'by judgement of the eye.'[10] 'Beauty itself doth of itself persuade/The eyes of men without an orator.'[11] So the eye alone is sufficient: there is no need for words. Architecture is indeed a visual art in the sense that it can only be fully understood and appreciated through the eye. Judging buildings or designs of buildings is largely a matter for the eye. An informed eye knows a beautiful building; and by an 'informed eye' I mean an eye that can 'read' the plan and section of a building and that, in looking at a completed building, can understand its organization, function and construction. I also mean an eye that can appreciate purely aesthetic qualities of scale, composition, silhouette, proportion, rhythm and how the building fits into its surroundings. To prove that a beautiful building is instantly recognizable, l shall compare two designs for the same power station at Bexley on a site on the south bank of the river Thames. The site is not normally thought of as an historic setting, but a greenfield site is just as much a context as a built-up urban area, and every site has a history. Whether on a greenfield site or in urban surroundings, the new buildings must undeniably be designed in a manner that is appropriate to the site, circumstances and function, but this must not exclude original and innovative architecture on the cutting edge of the art, like the Palace of Westminster, the Lloyd's Building or the Millennium Dome, structures, which all have been reviled as new designs. Context, or the need for integration, is only one of a number of factors, and to set too much store by it could

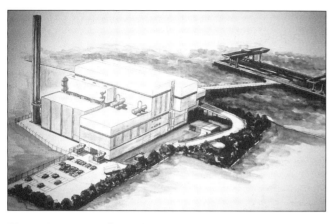

Figure 8.13: Design for Bexley Power Station, H and G Engineering.

Figure 8.14: Design for Bexley Power Station, Arup Associates.

deny the opportunity of innovation and excitement in architecture.

The first design for the power station was by H and G Engineering *(Figure 8.13)*. It had at its core a concrete structure surrounding the incinerator and its protected access routes. Although apparent on the elevations, this structure lay buried under an incoherent assembly of 'boxes', steel-framed structures clad with coloured aluminium sheeting, which provided the package for all the parts of the power station except the flue stacks and jetty. The Royal Fine Art Commission found the design unacceptable and wished to see a new proposal that acknowledged the nature of the site with a beautiful object in the landscape. It believed that this would require change in the form of the building and to its internal functions.

The Royal Fine Art Commission's suggestion that a designer of proven capability be asked to develop a new design was accepted by the client. The second design, by the architects Arup Associates *(Figure 8.14)*, was the result of reconsidering the relationship between the different parts, improving their operational efficiency and at the same time giving them a sense of unity and visual order. Only two-thirds of the plant is enclosed in the new design, while the cooling towers and flue stacks, with their closely related washing and filtering elements, remain outside and free-standing. The enclosure consists largely of a silver-anodized aluminium sheet roof, which is shaped to a tight curve for both economy and elegance.

Conclusion

The qualities pertaining to beauty that I have outlined – truth, integrity, simplicity, harmony – are neither exhaustive nor exclusive. Such qualities are found in buildings that time and consensus have declared beautiful, but a design possessing all these qualities will not necessarily result in a beautiful building. The architect of the building also has to be a good architect – the creative mastermind who can bring all the disparate parts together into an indivisible whole. It is possible, as I have tried to show in my book *What Makes a Good Building?*, to derive criteria from these qualities – criteria in the sense of principles or standards that things are judged by, rather than guidelines or rules, which imply direction by some outside authority. Criteria are more easily seen as self-imposed. They are objective values exhibiting facts that are not coloured by the feelings or opinions of the person making a judgement.

In assessing a design or a building one must look for quality and not for a particular style. Style is a matter of taste. It is possible to be objective about quality; taste, on the other hand, remains largely subjective – a matter of personal feelings or opinions. Quality is also enduring, while taste and fashions change. Though indefinable, quality, like a beautiful building, is immediately recognizable.

In the end what makes a beautiful building is a good brief, a good client and a good architect – in other words, enlightened architectural patronage. To achieve a beautiful building requires great effort and passionate commitment. The answer lies in the quality of the architecture and in the patron who is prepared to search for quality and take risks. 'If you have two loaves,' goes the Japanese proverb, 'sell one and buy a lily.'

References

1   KEATS, John, *Letters,* (ed. M B Forman, 1935) 98, To George and Georgiana Keats, 16 Dec. 1818–4 Jan. 1819.
2   *Ibid.* 31, To Benjamin Bailey, 22 Nov. 1819.
3   KEATS, John, 'Ode on a Grecian Urn', 1820.
4   VENTURI, Robert, *Complexity and Contradiction in Architecture,* Architectural Press, 1977.
5   EMERSON, Ralph Waldo, *Essays,* xii 'Art'.
6   LAUGIER, Marc-Antoine, *Essai sur l'architecture,* 1753.
7   Quoted by John Bailey in 'Why we chose James Kelman', *The Times,* 12 October 1994.
8   ROWE, Colin, 'Chicago frame', *The Architectural Review,* November 1956.
9   STRAVINSKY, Igor, *The Poetics of Music,* Harvard University Press, 1974, p.32.
10 SHAKESPEARE, William, *Love's Labour's Lost,* Act I, scene ii.
11 SHAKESPEARE, William, *The Rape of Lucrece,* l.29.

Examples of good practice, 1961–98

Paul Velluet *English Heritage*

That a regard for context and an understanding and appreciation of the past need pose no threat to architectural creativity and excellence, and that a new building can make a positive and distinct contribution to an historic setting, are demonstrated in numerous projects in diverse locations throughout the country.

The following projects, grouped by building type, represent a personal selection of relevant and sound examples of good practice completed in recent years. Importantly, it is not intended to be an exhaustive and comprehensive schedule, but simply a list of schemes that may be seen as offering inspiration and encouragement to the cause of good architecture in historic settings.

Residential projects

1 Private housing at The Retreat, Richmond, by John Darbourne.

2 Private housing at The Circle/Queen Elizabeth Street/Shad Thames, Bermondsey, London, SE1 by CZWG.

3 Social housing at Mercers' House, Islington, London, N1, by John Melvin.

4 Private house at 60 Kew Green, Kew, Surrey, by John Darbourne.

5 Almshouses at Hickey's Almshouses, Sheen Road/St Mary's Grove, Richmond, by Initiatives in Design.

6 Broadwall: social housing at Coin Street/Upper Ground, Lambeth, London, SE1, by Liftschutz Davidson Design.

7 Apartment building at China Wharf, Mill Street, Bermondsey, London, SE1, by CZWG; and new footbridge across St Saviour's Dock, Bermondsey, London SE1, by Nicholas Lacey.

8 Housing, office and retail development at Horselydown Square and Anchor Square, Horselydown Lane, Gainsford Street, Bermondsey, London SE1, by Wickham and Associates.

9 25 flats at nos. 78-79 Ashmill Street, London, NW1, by Jeremy Dixon.

2

2

5

Other earlier schemes

10 Infill House, Lansdowne Crescent, Notting Hill, London, W11 by Darbourne and Darke.

11 Flats for the Crown Estate at Crown Reach, Millbank, Pimlico, London, SW1 by Nicholas Lacey and Maguire and Murray.

12 Housing, Lanark Road, Maida Vale, London, W9 by Jeremy Dixon.

13 Housing for Westminster City Council at Lillington Gardens, Pimlico, London, SW1, by Darbourne and Darke.

14 Nos. 44-46, Huntsworth Mews, London, NW1.

6   7

Transport-related projects

15 Liverpool Street Station, London, EC2: Part reconstruction and rehabilitation, by British Rail Architecture and Design Group.

16 Eurostar Terminal at Waterloo Station, Lambeth, London, SE1, by Nicholas Grimshaw and Partners.

17 New footbridge across St Saviour's Dock, Bermondsey, London, SE1 by Nicholas Lacey.

8   11

University, college and school projects

18 Magdalen College, Oxford: The Grove Buildings Quadrangle by Demetri Porphyrious Associates.

19 The Burrell's Field Development for Trinity College, 56-62, Grange Road, Cambridge by MacCormac Jamieson Prichard.

20 The Stevens Building for the Royal College of Art, Jay Mews, Kensington, London, SW7, by John Miller and Partners.

21 The Sainsbury Building, Worcester College, Oxford, by MacCormac, Jamieson, Prichard.

22 Extension building at Richmond College, Queen Road, Richmond by Anthony Turrell.

23 Blue Boar Court, Trinity College, Cambridge, by MacCormac, Jamieson, Prichard.

24 The Maitland Robinson Library, Downing College, Cambridge, by Erith and Terry.

25 Library extension, St John's College, Cambridge, by Edward Cullinan.

26 Post-graduate Study Centre, Darwin College, Cambridge, by Jeremy Dixon, Edward Jones.

15   20

22   35

27 Quincentenary Library, Jesus College, Cambridge, by Shalev and Evans.

28 The Bowra Building, Wadham College, Oxford, by MacCormac, Jamieson, Prichard.

29 Hall of Residence for St Peter's College, Oxford, by Marcus Beale.

30 The Garden Quad, St John's College, Oxford, by MacCormac, Jamieson, Prichard.

31 New Kitchen and Junior Common Room, Magdalen College, Oxford, by Maguire and Murray.

32 Luxmore House, The King's School, Canterbury, by Maguire and Murray.

39

40

Other earlier schemes

33 Extension to the Royal College of Music, Prince Consort Road, South Kensington, London, SW7 by Casson and Conder.

34 New Building, Brasenose College, Oxford, by Powell and Moya.

35 The University Library, Palace Green, Durham City, by George Pace.

36 The Cripps Building, St John's College, Cambridge by Powell and Moya.

37 Dunelm House/The Students Union Building, Old Elvet, Durham City, by Dick Raines of the Architects' Co-partnership.

38 The Senior Combination Room, Downing College, Cambridge, by Howell, Killick, Patridge and Amis.

41

44

Cultural, ecclesiastical and sports projects

39 Westminster Cathedral, Cathedral Piazza/Ashley Place, London, SW1: The St Paul's Bookshop, by Peter Tigg Partnership.

40 Vaughan House, 46, Francis Street, London, SW1: Diocesan offices by Robert O'Hara.

41 The Royal Opera House Development, Covent Garden, London, WC2 by Jeremy Dixon, Ed Jones, BDP.

42 Lord's Cricket Ground, St John's Wood Road, London, NW1: The Mound Stand by Michael Hopkins and Partners.

43 Lord's Cricket Ground, St John's Wood, London, NW1: New stand by Nicholas Grimshaw and Partners.

44 The Anstruther Wing, The London Library, No. 7, Duke Street St James's, London, SW1: New

47

47

50

library extension and café/restaurant, by Michael Morrisson and Paul Vonberg of Purcell Miller Tritton and Partners.

45 Fountains Abbey, Studley Royal Park, Ripon, North Yorkshire: New Visitors Centre for English Heritage, by Edward Cullinan.

46 St Augustine's Abbey, Canterbury: New Visitors's Centre for English Heritage, by Van Heyningen and Haward.

47 The Christian Science Church Reading Room, Sheen Road, Richmond, by David Chipperfield.

48 St John the Baptist Church Hall, Pinner, Middlesex, by Weston Williamson.

49 The Globe Theatre, Bankside, London, SE1, by Pentagram Cedric Price and Peter McCurdy.

50 Studio cinema, Retreat Road, Richmond, by John Darbourne.

51 The Sackler Galleries, The Royal Academy/ Burlington House, Piccadilly, London, W1, by Sir Norman Foster and Partners and Julian Harrap.

52 The Princess of Wales Conservatory, The Royal Botanic Gardens Kew, by PSA Architects.

53 The Tower Bridge Visitors' Centre, Tower Bridge, London, E1, by Michael Squire Associates.

54 St Paul's Church and Centre, Half Acre, Brentford, Middlesex: rebuilding by Michael Blee Design.

55 Demountable ticket office for visitors to Buckingham Palace, Green Park, London SW1 by Michael Hopkins and Partners.

Other earlier schemes

56 Extension to the Theatre Royal, York, by Patrick Gwynne.

57 New church and other buildings at St Mary's Abbey, West Malling, Kent by Robert Maguire and Keith Murray.

58 The Royal College of Physicians, 11 St Andrew's Place, Regent's Park, London, NW1, by Denys Lasdun and Partners.

59 New Bell House at Chester Cathedral, by George Pace.

60 New chapel for Scargill House, Wharfedale, by George Pace.

61 Henley Royal Regatta Headquarters, Henley, by The Terry Farrell Partnership.

62 St Mary's Parish Church, Church Road, Barnes,

52

53

63

64

65

66

London, SW13: rebuilding after fire damage, by Edward Cullinan, Mark Beadle and Alan Short.

63 All Saint's Parish Church, Church Street, Isleworth, Middlesex: rebuilding, by Michael Blee.

64 The Queen Elizabeth Conference Centre, Broad Sanctuary, Westminster, London, SW1, by Powell and Moya.

65 The Turner Museum extension to The Tate Gallery, Millbank, London, SW1 by James Stirling, Michael Wilford and Associates.

69

Governmental, administrative and commercial projects

66 No. 3, Wardour Street, London, W1: retail and office building by Proun Architects.

67 Nos 20-22 Bedfordbury/Hop Gardens, Covent Garden, WC2: office building by Dick Dickinson of the Rolfe Judd Group.

68 Nos. 5-13, Palace Street, London, SW1: offices, by Dick Dickinson of the Rolfe Judd Group.

69 Nos. 2-4 Cork Street, London, W1: offices and showroom by Dick Dickinson of Rolfe Judd, Architects.

72   74

70 New public lavatories and florist's shop for The Royal Borough of Kensington and Chelsea Council, Westbourne Grove/Colville Road, London, W11, by CZWG.

71 The House Mill Museum and Miller's House Visitor Centre, Three Mill Lane, Bromley-by-Bow, London, E3, by Julian Harrap.

72 Improvements to Smithfield Market, London, EC1, by HLM Architects.

73 Conversion of Billingsgate Market, Lower Thames Street, London, EC3, by The Richard Rogers Partnership.

75

74 Office building at no. 4 Babmaes Street, St James's, London, SW1, by Fletcher Priest.

75 New headquarters office building at no. 60 Victoria Embankment, Tudor Street, John Carpenter Street and Carmalite Street, London, EC4, by BDP Architects.

76 Channel 4 Headquarters, 124, Horseferry Road, London, SW1, by The Richard Rogers Partnership.

77 New office and retail development on Villiers Street, London, WC2, by The Terry Farrell Partnership.

76   78

78 Bracken House, Cannon Street/Queen Victoria Street/Friday Street, London, EC4; part redevelopment and conversion by Michael Hopkins and Partners.

79 Inland Revenue Centre, Castle Meadow Road, Nottingham by Michael Hopkins and Partners.

Other earlier schemes

80 Embassy of the Federal German Republic, Chesham Place, Belgravia, London, SW1 by Dr Ing and Mrs Ing Betz with W M Saunders.

81 Office building at No. 6A, The Green, Richmond, by Darbourne and Darke.

82 Office building at No. 1, Finsbury Avenue, London, EC2 by Arup Associates.

83 Map House, St James's Street/St James's Place, London, SW1, by Triad Architects.

84 Office building at 4 and 5, Park Place and Arlington Street, St James's London, SW1, by the Mike Trickett of the Rolfe Judd Group.

85 Office building at 68, Cornhill, London, EC3, by Dick Dickinson of the Rolfe Judd Group.

86 Office and residential buildings on Richmond Riverside, Richmond, Surrey, by Erith and Terry.

87 The Comyn Ching Triangle; Conversion and redevelopment of site bounded by Shelton Street, Mercer Street and Monomouth Street, Covent Garden, London, WC2, by Terry Farrell and Partners.

88 Nos. 25-26, Pall Mall/No. 26, St James's Square, London, SW1: office building by Frederick Gibberd, Coombe and Partners.

89 Office building at nos 35-38 Chancery Lane/Cursitor Street, London, WC2, by BDP.

90 Richmond House, Whitehall/Derby Gate/New Scotland Yard, London, SW1.

91 Office building for the Department of Health and Social Security by Whitfield and Partners.

80

82

81

83

85

86

90

Section 3
Inside the mind of the designer

'Buildings .... live together like people, with occasional quarrels, mild bickerings, constant compromise, respect for individuals, plus the odd flight of passion or fancy. To search out, analyze and enrich this pattern demands an unusual degree of sophisticated insight and awareness. Gordon Cullen has suggested that there should be a new profession of 'Conceptors', men who can evaluate the nature of the scene and then convert it into a concept within a framework of which new buildings can comfortably (or energetically) sit....' Sir Hugh Casson, 1976.

When Sir Hugh Casson wrote these words in his essay in the seminal book on building conservation The Future of the Past, it was all part of the continuing campaign at that time to raise public and professional awareness of the importance of conserving the historic environment along with a sensitive approach to the design of new buildings. However, little did he realize that at the same time there was a generation of architects who perhaps can be termed 'conceptors' emerging from within the profession itself.

This section brings together some of those 'conceptors', leading practitioners in Europe, who give a unique insight into their approach towards designing for the historic environment. In many cases their work is not normally associated with historic settings and some were brought up with the tenets of the Modern Movement but, along with other influences, their experience is translated into designs that sit comfortably (or energetically) into the historic environment.

John Wells-Thorpe, from his perspective as both architect and client, argues strongly for the trust of the building owner and the designer. Edward Cullinan, who has designed new buildings in historic settings for most of his career, advocates a policy that does not unduly 'kow-tow' to the historic environment. Richard MacCormac gives a fascinating insight into his approach by revealing his architectural heroes and influences. He also stresses, as does Spencer de Grey, the importance of enlightened clients. John Lyall and Pi de Bruijn with illustrations from vastly contrasting buildings in different European cities show how they carefully knit together historic areas of cities bringing new life with vibrant new insertions.

There is no single solution; each case has to be considered in both its cultural and physical context along with the need for a delicate balance between protecting the historic fabric and creating up-to-date facilities for new uses.

From Bauhaus to Boilerhouse 10

John Wells-Thorpe Architect. Chairman,
South Downs Health NHS Trust

Summary

John Wells-Thorpe is a respected practitioner who was brought up with the Modern Movement but also, through time spent at the British School in Rome, as a student of the best of the past. In this chapter he reflects on where Modernism perhaps lost touch with public acceptability and the resultant shallowness of 'contextualism' as designers scramble to meet the approval of planning committees and public participation.

He reflects on the over-emphasis of the Modern Movement on 'the shock of the new', and recognizes the causes of public reaction. However, the result has often been a pendulum swing to historic pastiche and a veneer of historicism. Through case studies of both his own work and that of others, an argument is made for a variety of approaches: 'straight reproduction', as with the reconstruction of the Chamber of the House of Commons; the reworking of Classicism, as at the new library at Jesus College, Cambridge by Evans and Shalev; to I M Pei's glass pyramid at the Louvre in Paris, which provides an excellent example of harmony through contrast. There is a recognition that no one response is correct. The appropriate response depends on the circumstances and may vary from straight reproduction (the copy) through contrast, to synthesis. Even having chosen the appropriate design strategy, the success of the outcome depends upon the perceptions and sensitivity of the designer, which cannot be regulated.

In conclusion the author, reflecting on his role in the last five years as Chairman of a hospital trust and client for a major capital programme, despairs about the influence of journalists, critics and politicians who have become 'self-appointed custodians of our cultural conscience.' He argues for the strong moral position of the building owner, who needs the building to give 'shelter and security for a specific activity'. Trust the responsible building owner working with the sensitive designer and aim to 'avoid absolutes, allow for plurality, risk the occasional mistake, reject mediocrity, resist superficiality, and design with sincerity.'

The passage of time

Two totally unrelated events that I recall are separated by over thirty years, but they both have a bearing on attitudes towards the siting of new buildings in older surroundings. Shortly after the Second World War, as a student spending some time at the British School in Rome, I used a good deal of time looking at buildings of historical significance that have found their way into all the history books. One of these was Bramante's *Tempietto* situated in the cortile of the Church of *San Pietro* in Montorio. The *Tempietto* is sufficiently well recorded and described elsewhere so I shall concentrate on the aspect of it that struck me most after having marvelled at Bramante's gem itself. The surprise, of course, was to find this beautiful little Renaissance building jammed into the relatively small cortile of a church whose style sprang from an earlier century. *San Pietro* is a very ordinary building of an ordinary size, and the sudden addition of this stylistic interloper, however magnificent in itself, has always puzzled me.

Many years later I was asked to prepare a master plan for the long-term development of Lancing College in Sussex where some of the most significant work had been undertaken by R C Carpenter in the nineteenth century. By this time I had become so sensitive about introducing new work to older settings that I can recall saying to a meeting of the governing council that one of my objectives in siting the new buildings was to 'spend several million pounds of your money and have nothing to show for it.' Such was the completeness of the original architectural grouping when seen from the east that it seemed important to play down or even conceal the new additions.

My thoughts now, therefore, are concerned with why this change in attitude should take place and to examine whether or not the swing of opinion has gone too far. If it has, to try and identify what has prompted this reaction. In selecting the title 'Bauhaus to Boilerhouse' I chose a form of shorthand for the space of over fifty years that separates the beginnings of the Modern Movement from the recently

Figure 10.1: Embassy Court, Hove. 1930s apartments by Wells Coates.

published designs by Daniel Libeskind for the new wing to the Victoria and Albert Museum in London. Obviously, a great deal has happened in this half-century, particularly the change in attitude towards the surroundings of new work; it therefore seems a useful way to examine the attitudinal shift and the reasons behind it.

Those who have chronicled the rise and fall of the Modern Movement have identified two of its failings among its many conspicuous successes. The first limitation involves an almost complete lack of dialogue with the end user – and this is no doubt where persistent assertions of architectural arrogance stem from. The second limitation involves the almost complete and deliberate absence of any consideration for physical context *(Figure 10.1)*. Modern Movement architects, driven presumably by some crusading zeal, seemed impervious to context and became blindly assertive over what they were constructing afresh.

Reverting to South Kensington, it has to be remembered that the Victoria and Albert Museum is not a single building, but a combination of structures accumulated at different times, mainly during the second half of the nineteenth and early part of the twentieth century. It should be recalled that there is an historical precedent for a building of some sort on the vacant site; a project (un-executed) was prepared for this land in 1868. Libeskind describes his current proposal as 'a labyrinth of discovery' and as 'the spiral of art and history.' He describes the entire manifestation as 'an organizational *leit-motif*' *(Figure 10.2)*. The architect says that the pattern of polychrome terracotta tiles is a direct reference to *The Grammar of Ornament*[1] by Owen Jones, and whatever else history will have to say of this proposal, it certainly reflects great courage on the part of the Trustees for giving it their backing.

Figure 10.2: Victoria and Albert Museum, London. Model of proposal – since updated – on the site of the former Boilerhouse by Daniel Libeskind, 1996.

They used not to care

The growth of the national preservation movement and the role of pressure groups since Victorian times is well described in Michael Hunter's book, *Preserving the Past: the rise of heritage in modern Britain.*[2] A significant aspect of this study is that its scope only begins in the nineteenth century. Before that it did not appear to be a topic that anyone considered worthy of separate discussion; we shall see later why this new awareness has come upon us. It is well recorded that most of our great cathedrals grew organically with the possible exception of Salisbury, which looks more of a piece and in very general terms gives the impression of having been built, as Pevsner describes it, 'all in one go.'[3] However, taking other cathedrals, for example Norwich, you will find Romanesque first and Gothic later, with no indication that there was any obligation on the part of the designer to be influenced by what was being added to or what was adjacent (*Figure 10.3*).

Figure 10.3: Former St Paul's Cathedral, London. Suggested portico by Inigo Jones, 1658 is an equally vivid example of casually mixed styles.

In 1726 Nicholas Hawksmoor designed a Corinthian altar for York Minster. Some splendid pen and wash proposals still exist in the British Library and the York Minster Library giving a very full indication of what Hawksmoor proposed.

But they do care now

It is clear that something must have happened that has led to contextual design becoming an important issue, and we need to ask why. It is fairly easy to guess that, like the preservation of old buildings, the question of harmonization stems from a popular and widespread rejection of the Modern Movement. Because so many of the benefits of the Modern Movement are now taken for granted, for example light, air, space, technology, transparency and flexibility, it is customary to disparage all that followed the 1930s and point only to its failings. The rejection of much modern architecture is also reflected in the use of retained façades of older buildings (many of which are of very slender merit) and the demand that the new building should be jammed in behind, thus concealed from public gaze. If one pauses for a moment, it is glaringly obvious that such practice is functionally limiting, structurally perverse, economically irresponsible and intellectually bankrupt. It seems as if twentieth-century technology is useful in its place as long as it does not show. The recent restoration of Little Moreton Hall in Cheshire shows how steel warren trusses are inserted to prop up an entirely inadequate and outworn timber structure, and have been sufficiently well concealed to give the impression that the structural integrity of the existing building has still been maintained.

However, the architecture of the last five or ten years has become more 'approachable', and a larger number of people are dropping their earlier hostility. It would be interesting to re-run twentieth-century history and have the principal architectural characters in the 1930s played by, for example, Sir Michael Hopkins, Richard MacCormac, Edward Cullinan and Leonard Mannaseh, designing as they do now. Perhaps the public alienation would never have taken place and, in all probability, no-one would have needed to invent the word 'contextualism'.

Journalists invariably reiterate received opinion, which quickly falls into stereotype when they discuss modern architecture. For example, Sir Norman Foster's plan for the Millau viaduct over the valley of the Tarn caused *Le Figaro* to describe it as 'a grand triumph for technical thinking over cultural thinking' – very French! And the design by Sir Michael Hopkins for the Queen's Building at Emmanuel College, Cambridge was described recently by an architectural historian who should know better as 'a trolley bus jammed in the back yard, built with expensive stone, made to look like chipped plywood.' Seen from another viewpoint, looseness of description can also be guaranteed to produce looseness of design. When Leon Krier was asked to design an urban extension to Dorchester at Poundbury, it was to be 'in sympathy with the style and layout of traditional west Dorset.' Descriptive imprecision of this order is bound to muddle the creative process, and the compromised results are there for all to see.

The role of public participation has become significant since the Skeffington Report nearly thirty years ago, and it is not difficult to see how valuable is such participation. Clearly, because we live in a democratic society, there should be every reasonable opportunity taken to involve the public who are probably paying indirectly for the new project, or at least will have to look at it in the future. However, if one examined all proposals on this basis then one would merely end up with the lowest common denominator of popular architectural expression.

To assess its usefulness in the light of comments received from the public on the original National Gallery extension competition, one only has to remember that the design that attracted most criticism (by Richard Rogers) was the very same design that simultaneously attracted most praise from other members of the public. As a result of this attitude we often have to put up with a form of tokenism, which does not really advance the case other than making everyone feel a great deal more politically correct. It may be no coincidence that the new Heywood Hill prize for a lifetime's achievement in books is to be judged on 'accessibility and readability.' This may annoy critics, but it is yet another feeler to a puzzled public who believe that they have lost touch with many manifestations of late twentieth-century culture.

The stirrings of conscience

It is worthwhile to look back and see when post-war architects began to feel, probably quite unconsciously, the need for a greater awareness of the setting in which their new buildings were to sit. In the early 1950s Sir Basil Spence designed some fishermen's cottages on the coast at Dunbar, which had a close affinity with local vernacular but were unmistakably of their own time. In Essex, Tayler & Green designed some excellent low-cost housing that was quintessentially of its time and place and was a beautifully measured understatement, entirely appropriate for its location. In the early 1960s the Civic Trust began to make awards for buildings that acknowledged their surroundings, and at Hastings in the old town, Sir William Holford's practice was asked to provide housing infill to areas ravaged by the War and subsequent depression. Holford asserted that they could be as modern as they liked as long as they observed the 'scale, proportion and materials' of their surroundings. Looking at it thirty years on it seems an entirely apt response.

At about the same time I was restoring the oldest secular building in Brighton, the home of one Deryk Carver, brewer and Protestant martyr, which dates back to 1555. Having done that, I was asked to design a block of offices immediately next door. The very essence of office design presupposes unimpeded horizontal floor plates, but the treatment given was essentially vertical with more than a nod in the direction of the net-drying sheds of Hastings and the waterside buildings on the Sussex coast *(Figure 10.4)*. In 1950 *The Architectural Review* produced one of its excellent special issues devoted to 'The Functional Tradition,'[4] which gave great encouragement to consider new projects taking inspiration from the nautical tradition. Looking back, it seems that examples such as this were in a minority. More aggressive responses not far removed from Brutalism were shortly to come. This no doubt put the final nail in the coffin of modern architecture.

Figure 10.4: Black Lion Street, Brighton. Offices by John Wells-Thorpe, 1972.

The long shadow of the theme park

As stylistic invention floundered following the minimalist aesthetic of the Modern Movement, a number of hastily considered alternatives began to appear and quick and 'easy' design answers were resorted to. It became common to respond to client pressure for early planning permission by designing a broadly populist building that would attract consent, or at least be sufficiently uneventful to avoid criticism. It was not surprising that the major brewers and supermarket operators had their architects turning to the theme park for inspiration, either because they actually believed that this degree of escapism was appropriate or because they just gave way to pressure to get on with the job. Examples abound of schizophrenic designs where air-conditioned interiors are shrouded in two-dimensional period dress.

Quite clearly, the escapism so well devised by Disneyland has a very proper place in the leisure industry and no-one is arguing for its exclusion on the grounds of vulgarity or an inadequate theoretical base, but one has to take exception to sloppy thinking getting in the way of more serious design considerations, which have a significant and lasting place in our built environment.

A closer look: some case studies

Building juxtaposition

In the late 1960s the town hall in Hove by Alfred Waterhouse was burnt down, despite being described by Pevsner as 'so red, so hard, so imperishable'! The conflagration was almost complete and permission was sought to design new and much larger premises. I was commissioned to undertake the design and, looking back, I was given far more freedom than ever would be the case today, not just in being allowed to demolish a small part of the building that had remained intact after the fire, but also in choosing a form of architectural expression of the moment and not being in any way inhibited by the aesthetic opinions that are so frequently imposed by well-meaning but poorly informed clients and planning committees.

The contents of the new town hall were not a straight replacement for the old accommodation, but reflected a very ambitious vision for the future. The first decision I made was to visit with the clients the Netherlands and West Germany to see what had already been accomplished in town hall design. Central to this enterprise was a visit to Dudok's Hilversum town hall, which incidentally has now been magnificently restored and is carefully and conscientiously revered by local inhabitants.

The resulting design was essentially of its time and could be regarded as 'mainstream' *(Figure 10.5)*. However, I recognized that it was important to choose an external cladding material that harmonized much better with the surroundings than did the red brick Alfred Waterhouse building. Secondly, where the new town

Figure 10.5: Hove Town Hall (linking wing). Civic centre by John Wells-Thorpe, 1974.

hall abutted existing and undamaged residential terraces, the scale of the building was reduced to an identical height, so that it was seen to grow out of its surroundings rather than be imposed upon them. These days such considerations are totally forgotten by the local inhabitants and it falls into the predictable category of being out out of date and is commonly disliked as a building.

When Erno Goldfinger designed his own home in Hampstead at No. 2 Willow Road, he probably had no idea that it would subsequently be preserved by the National Trust. It certainly would not obtain planning permission today and yet when Pevsner saw it in its context he observed 'Here is the contemporary style in an uncompromising form, yet by the use of brick and by sheer scale the terrace goes infinitely better with the Georgian past of Hampstead than anything Victorian.'[5]

In the hands of an internationally accomplished architect, one occasionally comes across a solution for which there is no precedent and where a subtle restraint is concealed within what appears to be an overt technological solution. The glass pyramid by I M Pei at the Louvre in Paris is an excellent example of harmony through contrast. It legitimizes the value of contrast and is as good an indication as one will ever find of how a single brilliant structure produces an uncompromising solution that looks absolutely right *(Figure 10.6)*.

In more recent years, in the context of Cambridge common-room opinion , it was not surprising that severe constraints were imposed upon Evans & Shalev when designing the new library for Jesus College. All credit must go to the Master, the

Figure 10.6: Le Louvre, Paris. Pyramidical roof to underground extension by I M Pei.

distinguished archaeologist Lord Renfrew, in selecting these designers for this commission, which is a subtle and skilful reworking of Classicism within the context of the College's architectural setting but avoids looking like a compromise *(Figure 10.7)*.

Siting and setting

Much has been written and no doubt much more will be said about an appropriate setting for St Paul's Cathedral when the Paternoster scheme is finally decided. When Sir William Holford designed the block layout on the blitzed areas adjacent to St Paul's in the 1960s he maintained, as others have done since, that the best views of the cathedral are the partial ones like that up Ludgate Hill where only half the west front can be seen. The cathedral is best seen from close to, and at all costs Holford maintained that one should avoid anything approaching Mussolini's answer to the approach to St Peter's, Rome along the reconstructed *Via del Conciliazione*, which is long, boring and unimaginative. He also maintained, and in this assertion he was supported by Sir Basil Spence, that the buildings surrounding St Paul's should not be a pale copy of the Baroque style. In a supporting letter in the press Spence said in effect, if you have a diamond of great price you do not set it in artificial diamonds, but you contrast it with a ruby. Clearly, there is great validity in the argument, even if the ordinariness of the resulting office blocks was a great disappointment. Wren accepted that his masterpiece would be set in a confined and

Figure 10.7: Library for Jesus College, Cambridge by Evans and Shalev, 1995.

irregular space, roughly the shape of the old medieval churchyard, and the impending solution for this area of world importance will demand a mixture of boldness and intuition given to few.

Straight reproduction

Clearly there are circumstances in which straight reproduction is a legitimate and obvious answer to the problem and, with the benefit of hindsight, the reconstruction of the Chamber of the House of Commons after the Second World War at the behest of Sir Winston Churchill is probably an appropriate response, notwithstanding the very cogent arguments advanced by James Richards in favour of an entirely new Chamber. In today's world, the reconstruction of two opera houses recently ravaged by fire in Venice and Barcelona respectively fall into this category because of the overwhelming physical and emotional constraints imposed upon the designers concerned.

A clash of cultures

In a multi-cultural society within a shrinking world, it would not be fitting to leave this discussion without reference to the impact of other cultures upon the design process. History has already demonstrated the inadequacies, both functional and symbolic, in Lutyens' New Delhi and in Le Corbusier's Chandigarh. All this is not to say that when, for example, the British government intervened in Bombay to build a number of well-known public buildings it should have indulged in Royal Pavilion, Brighton pastiche. Interesting architectural hybrids are beginning to emerge as a result of the fusion of cultures. Casson Conder, in their design for the

Ismaili Centre in Kensington, manage to assimilate the very essence of its culture without descending into pastiche. This is a highly intelligent and sensitive response to an unusual and demanding problem.

Theory and practice

If we ask ourselves how to design a building in context, it is probably impossible to teach. Ruskin in *The Seven Lamps of Architecture* says 'the man who has eye and intellect will invent beautiful proportions, and cannot help it; but he can no more tell us how to do it than Wordsworth could tell us how to write a sonnet, or than Scott could tell us how to plan a romance.'[6] In other words, the skill is intuitive. This is borne out by what Geoffrey Scott says in *The Architecture of Humanism*[7] where, in similar vein, he asserts 'no amount of reasoning will create, or can annul, an aesthetic experience; for the aim of the arts has not been logic, but delight'.

However, more fruitfully, I found the observation contained in the distinguished practitioner and academic Colin St John Wilson's *Architectural Reflections*[8] quoting T S Eliot's theory of the relationship between tradition and novelty, exceptional for its power and originality:

> What happens when a new work of art is created is something that happens simultaneously to all the works of art which preceded it. The existing monuments form an ideal order among themselves, which is modified by the introduction of the new (the really new) work of art among them. The existing order is complete before the new work arrives; for order to persist after the supervention of novelty, the whole existing order must be, if ever so slightly, altered; and so the relations, proportions, values of each work of art toward the whole are readjusted; and this is conformity between the old and the new. Whoever has approved this idea of order .... will not find it preposterous that the past is altered by the present as much as the present is directed by the past. And the [architect] who is aware of this will be aware of great difficulties and responsibilities.

Assessment and intuition

There is no finite conclusion; the debate goes on, not least of all because there is no one right way to integrate a new building into an historic setting. As we showed earlier from Ruskin and others, there are some things that cannot be taught. A feel for contextualism is most certainly a necessity, but it does not mean to say that, over the years, a number of valid solutions have not presented themselves. It may be worth while examining these and recognizing that each, in certain circumstances, can be appropriate or wrong.

The copy

There are situations where a conscientious and scholarly answer can satisfy most of the demands placed upon the designer and such examples have a place in the built environment. However, this model is all too easily mishandled for cynical reasons or out of sheer ignorance, and one is left with a cosmetic solution that falls into the same category as the breweries' 'Tudorbethan' roadhouses of the 1930s.

The contrast

Clearly this is, in terms of the current debate, the most interesting but at the same time the most demanding of architectural understanding. It entails some discipline as Holford suggested at Hastings in the 1960s but, as with the 'copy', it is equally capable of producing a disastrous result in the form of arrogant exhibitionism and does nothing to nurture balanced debate.

The synthesis

This solution, which entails almost as much intuitive skill as the contrast, can sometimes work, as demonstrated in the Evans & Shalev library at Cambridge, but like the other two approaches above, it can end as a weak and muddled compromise in inexperienced hands.

I can offer tentatively some considerations about contextualism that may at least prevent the worst sort of failure. Such considerations may include an asessment of:

- The extent of old surroundings, e.g: after the Blitz, at the Palace of Westminster, was the entire Lower House to be reconstructed or merely one or two broken pinnacles on the roof?

- The worth of old surroundings, e.g: are the neighbouring buildings all listed Grade I, or do they lack such distinction?

- The consistency of old surroundings, e.g: are you building in an area that is coherent and complete, or more fragmented?

- The uniqueness of old surroundings, e.g: is the neighbouring building the only example of its type, or is it typical of its species?

- The proximity of old surroundings, e.g: are the neighbouring structures near enough to be seen in the same sweep of the eye?

To conclude, there is no one approach. I would avoid absolutes; allow for plurality; risk the occasional mistake; reject mediocrity; resist superficiality; but design with sincerity.

Postscript

Having rather unexpectedly been cast in the role of a client with a major capital programme for the last five years, it has given me the opportunity to see the whole debate through the other end of the telescope. I sense in myself a growing impatience with self-appointed custodians of our cultural conscience, be they critics, journalists or politicians on the make. Beneath the surface there is a feeling that building ownership is a slightly tainted occupation, and words like 'developer' and 'landlord' come far too readily to mind when criticism is being mounted. It is therefore timely to remind ourselves why building owners own a building. It is usually to give shelter and security for a specific activity in which they are engaged, often with other people's money (tax payers in the public sector and shareholders in the private). They are therefore in a strong moral position to hold a priority view about what happens to that building both in the design process and in the period of subsequent use. There are many very responsible building owners who do not trumpet their achievements, but undertake their responsibilities with verve and conscientiousness. In the 1995-96 Annual Report for the Whitbread Group, we are reminded that 'it is a remarkable fact that the company owns and operates four times as many listed buildings open to the public than the National Trust. Taking care of the fabric of these buildings, along with their grounds, makes a major contribution to the national quality of life.'

In keeping with the title of this chapter, I give the last word to Lord Armstrong, Chairman of the Victoria and Albert Museum's Board of Trustees, in support of Daniel Libeskind's design. 'The V & A is already something of a medley of architectural styles, with which we have become so familiar that it no longer provokes comment.' He then concludes by asserting that 'the V & A is not just about the promotion of scholarship and the study of the history of design, important though both those purposes are. It exists also to encourage and display contemporary aspects of applied art and design.' Which is another way of saying that Ruskin was right all those years ago.

References

1. JONES, Owen, *The Grammar of Ornament*, Day, 1856.
2. HUNTER, Michael, *Preserving the Past: the rise of heritage in modern Britain*, Far Thrupp, Stroud, Alan Sutton, 1996.
3. PEVSNER, Sir Nikolaus, & CHERRY, Bridget, *The Buildings of England: Wiltshire*, Harmondsworth, Penguin Books, 1975.
4. 'The functional tradition' *The Architectural Review*, volume cvii, number 637, special number for January 1950.
5. PEVSNER, Nikolaus, *The Buildings of England: London except the cities of London and Westminster*, Harmondsworth, Penguin Books, 1952, p.196.
6. RUSKIN, John, *The Seven Lamps of Architecture*, Orpington, Allen, 1895, 6th edition.
7. SCOTT, Geoffrey, *The Architecture of Humanism: a study in the history of taste*, Methuen, 1961 (First published 1914).
8. WILSON, St John, *Architectural Reflections: studies in the philosophy and practice of architecture*, Oxford, Butterworth-Heinemann, 1992.

Contributing to historic settings without kow-towing

11

Edward Cullinan Edward Cullinan Architects

Summary

In section 2 of this book Paul Velluet presents an overview of the Acts and guidance that enable local authorities, government agencies and pressure groups to control planning decisions concerning new buildings in historic settings. As he points out, under the Planning (Listed Buildings and Conservation Areas) Act, 1990, when looking at proposals for new developments in historic settings, local authorities are formally required to give special attention to the desirability of 'preserving or enhancing' the character or appearance of a conservation area.

Edward Cullinan, who has designed new buildings in historic areas for the past 30 years, takes issue with some of these provisions. He considers that they are inhibitive to good modern design, mainly because those in control do not always have the necessary aesthetic sensibility to make good judgements and therefore settle for mediocrity.

Since his design for Minster Lovell Mill, 1967, which established his reputation for combining old and new, many commissions have followed for new buildings in historic or as he calls them, 'holy' places. In this chapter he discusses several of those designs, which cover a wide range of building types including small-scale housing developments (Leighton Crescent, Camden); the rebuilding of a medieval church destroyed by fire (St Mary's Barnes); the visitor centre for Fountains Abbey; large urban developments (Ludgate Hill); and educational buildings (Library for St John's College, Cambridge and Media Centre, Cheltenham). Through these buildings he discusses the elements that influence his approach, which is not to design replicas or use watered down components lifted from the past, but to extract and abstract the qualities of the historic surroundings in order to enhance them. He addresses the question of tradition in architecture and what it might mean in the late twentieth century, and ends with a message for the future.

The chapter stems from his lecture in York on 24 October 1996 with extracts from his book written with Kenneth Powell, **Edward Cullinan Architects,** *Academy Editions, 1995.*

Introduction

There are too many conservation areas in Britain. They inhibit the development of good modern architecture. They might not, if planning committees, government agencies and local pressure groups always had the aesthetic sensibility to be able to judge whether new buildings, however different, enhanced the conservation area or not. But many, quite naturally, do not have such peculiar sensibility and why should they? So they settle in the end for new buildings that are somewhat like the old buildings that surround them. They seldom ask for replicas, usually because they believe that there exists a mild mannered modern architecture composed of simplified or watered down components, lifted from the past. This is the architecture of kow-towing. Through weakening and mockery it insults both the past and the present, and enhances neither. Successful compositions need not depend on semi-sameness; contrast can be equally successful.

The examples of new buildings in historic settings that I will show are attempts to contribute to those settings in a positive, late twentieth-century manner; extracting and abstracting the qualities of the historic surroundings in order to enhance them. I shall do this in six sections using modern buildings by way of illustration:

- Solid and void: letting the sky in: Minster Lovell Mill

- Making a middle: Leighton Crescent

- Making a future for the past 1: Barnes Church

- Houses and gardens: RMC International headquarters

- Making a future for the past 2: Fountains Abbey

- Response, completion, crescendo: Ludgate Hill; St John's College, Cambridge; Media Centre, Cheltenham School of Art

Solid and void: letting the sky in

In cities you can be unaware of the sky; in good cities the walls are paramount, walls that combine to frame public places. In villages the sloping roofs are as apparent as the walls of the separate buildings, often more apparent, pitching away from one another to let the great sky down towards the ground between buildings.

Starting in 1967 we turned the buildings at Minster Lovell Mill, on the edge of the Cotswolds, into a conference centre. The plan of the mill as it was shows the L-shaped house (L), malt house (M), barn (B), and long drystone wall (D), all stretched out along the north side of the River Windrush, itself crossed by the base of the onetime water mill (W).

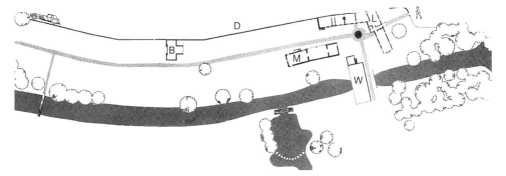

A section through the barn shows big doors on opposite sides of the building; it was T-shaped to keep the horses dry whilst the hay was being unloaded; the roof was dominant, letting the sky down. Here we extended the roofs of the barn downwards to make rooms that service the main seminar room in the barn top; we made the roof more dominant. Then we used the resulting section again to build another building beside it, which contains a returning stair that leads to a first floor, leading in turn to the main barn top seminar room. Study bedrooms cluster around the edge, beneath the extended roofs.

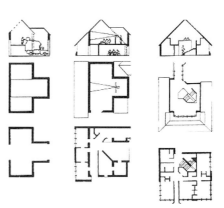

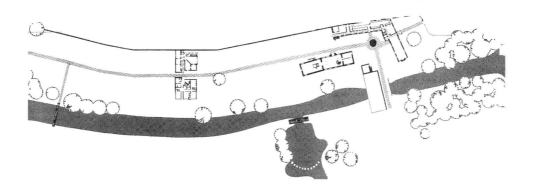

The combined composition sits atop a riverside terrace, beneath which are further study bedrooms, a termination.

Linking the barn complex to the L-shaped house are more study bedrooms. They are housed beneath stone covered roofs, derived from the barn complex, extended across the drystone wall without putting weight on it.

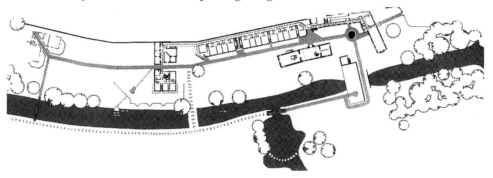

A further tiny development of this abstracted roofing system is a little cloister, which joins the study bedrooms to the barn, letting the sky down still.

There is not a so called 'Cotswold feature' in sight: no studded doors, no crotcheted chimneys, no coach lamps, no leaded lights, no dormers, no buttresses, no wobble. It is a late twentieth-century formal response to an historic situation, a response that learns from the divine moment of Cubism, a response that treats walls and roofs as planes, openings as cracks between planes, sticks as sticks crossing one another, elements as elements.

Figure 11.1: Minster Lovell Mill.

Making a middle

We designed and built the four houses and twelve flats at Leighton Crescent in Camden Town between 1974 and 1979.

The site plan shows the building in the middle of the Crescent. The rest of the Crescent is made up of late Victorian houses with bay windows and front steps and porticoes that you could buy out of a builder's merchant's catalogue in 1880. This was a very simple process of course – you went along and bought your bits and did your elevations; the plans were all completely standard and you got your house. Its a good big scale and very Victorian; the chimneys are very economical – you shared your chimneys with next door – and you had to keep them dry, in the middle of the house, because the buildings were also leaky.

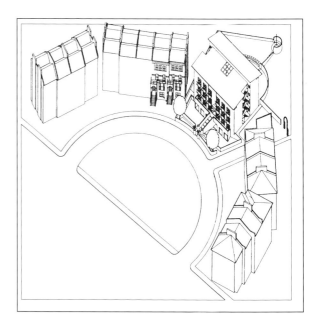

It was suggested to us that the best solution to building in this numinous setting would be to make single-storey dwellings that apparently disappeared, a common enough late twentieth-century nostalgic longing, which is impossible to achieve. Upon discovering this it was then proposed that we design a row of 3.6 m frontage town houses, which would have looked totally out of proportion to the Victorian ones on either side.

So we set about designing a building that could match up to its serious urban task of providing a centrepiece for the crescent. The solution was deceptively simple, it was to turn the lower floor houses and upper floor flats around sideways with bedroom and living room, joined or separate, side by side along the frontage. This allowed us to give each flat three large square French windows opening onto balconies 3 m apart vertically and horizontally, to produce a scale that could stack up to the Victorian surroundings. The entire horizontal fenestration of the top flats forms a negative version of the surrounding Victorian cornices.

Figure 11.2: Leighton Crescent.

Making a future for the past: 1

The Parish Church of St Mary's in Barnes, south London had all the qualities most likely to inspire nostalgia. Some parts were medieval; it was close to the village green, which had a duck pond with weeping willows, a litch gate and yew trees – it was and is a vital part of the collection of pieces that allows the population of this Victorian London suburb to refer to it as 'The Village' or 'Barnes Village'. It was an is an icon.

All parties agreed on a careful restoration of the medieval church. However, controversy rampaged through Barnes and far beyond, between two groups. The first, not trusting the architecture of the late twentieth century to rise to the occasion, wished to rebuild the whole church as it had been, though rather smoother. The second, led by the church council who represented most of the regular church-goers, wanted to make a building more suited to their present needs, and wanted Edward Cullinan Architects to do it. It is impossible to describe the heat that was raised around this particular parish pump – but the second group were very tenacious, very brave and mostly had their way. Now nearly everyone I meet in Barnes claims to be of this view.

The first sketch of the church shows how it had developed until 1978: a small medieval church with a twelfth-century nave, a thirteenth-century chancel, and a sixteenth-century tower. It had been reduced to the status of a south aisle for a large new nave and north aisle in the early part of this century. In the late 1970s there was a ferocious fire and the next sketch shows some of the bits that survived it more or less intact. The final sketches show how the church was recast, to restore the medieval church for daily use and to make a much larger nave to the north, reusing many old pieces in the process.

The medieval church was reroofed with steel and timber ridge trusses that grow out across the new parts to provide a unifying canopy over the whole composition, which has parts dating from the twelfth to the twentieth century; eight hundred years united beneath a single new coloured roof or interior sky.

Figure 11.3: The Parish Church of St Mary's, Barnes.

Houses and gardens

Between 1986 and 1990 we designed and built Ready Mix Concrete's headquarters at Thorpe in Surrey. The Romans established Londinium on the first substantial gravel banks as they sailed or rowed or floated on the tide up the River Thames. Further upstream, gravel and sand predominate over London clay, and here today are established sand and gravel pits from which come the raw materials for the concrete that rebuilds the city. These pits are filled in turn by rubble from demolished buildings and so on *ad infinitum*. Recently some of these pits have been turned into recreational lakes, and the largest of these is a kind of inland seaside created only a few miles out of London at Thorpe Park by the Ready Mix Concrete Company. Discretely distant from the frivolities of the park, the company had a site by a lake whose banks are nibbled by old-fashioned (therefore educational) sheep and whose surface is only disturbed (but quite frequently) by a re-created Mississippi stern wheeler.

On this site was a seventeenth-century Classical house, its stable block, and a late nineteenth-century Arts and Crafts villa, all listed, and two listed garden walls and many trees, all scheduled for preservation. All the new accommodation is placed within this framework, received from the past: offices for 200; foyer and restaurant; dining rooms; squash courts; gym; swimming pool; teaching rooms; bedrooms; laboratories; meeting and board rooms; and service rooms.

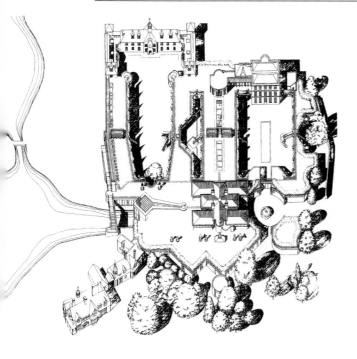

The red brick outside edge (framework) of houses and walls – itself an extension of the roadside walls in Thorpe Village – encompasses the site and is penetrated only by vital entry points. Within is a world made of fair-faced painted concrete, steel, hardwood and plate glass; gardens of grass, water, shrubs, trees and flowers; with gardens on top of and in between the buildings as courtyards. All the buildings are naturally lit, naturally ventilated, highly insulated and heavily built for temperature retention; in these ways they predict a future of low energy, ecological building.

Our main client was the terminally outspoken Chairman, John Camden. But of course you would expect a certain energy and directness from the man who had built the company from almost nothing to the largest of its kind on earth. When receiving a prize in the Whitehall Banqueting Hall, he let the world know that he thought architects were like lawyers, an unfortunate necessity. I loved that, for we are utterly necessary.

Figure 11.4: RMC Headquarters, Thorpe, Surrey.

Making a future for the past: 2

We designed and built the visitor's building at Fountains Abbey and Studley Royal between 1987 and 1992.

In the early eighteenth century the market crash known as the 'South Sea Bubble' ended the career of the Chancellor of the Exchequer. This was fantastic news for the development of landscape gardening, for he was banished to his Yorkshire estate of Studley Royal, next to the land on which Fountains Hall and the ruins of the abbey lay. Here, he and (probably) Colen Campbell with others, laid out the great gardens of Studley Royal. This resulted in an avenue that leads from an obelisk at the west end, towards the west front of Ripon Cathedral – four miles to the east – and the great water gardens in the Skell valley. From an upper lake, which curves round an artificial hill, two successive straight canals descend by waterfalls to a large lower lake that fills the valley floor. On either side of the canals, the old meanderings of

Site plan of Fountains Abbey and Studley Royal, September 1992.

the river – now cut off – are composed into formal and locally symmetrical settings of ponds and sculptures. Walking up from the large lake reveals a constant series of vistas and events that culminate in discovering the ruined abbey, half a kilometre away across another lake which curves round an artificial hill. But that is not all, for in addition to walking through the valley there are many look-outs one hundred feet above the valley floor with views across and down over the gardens. The final

Figure 11.5: The visitor centre at Fountains Abbey.

discovery is a distant view of the abbey from a small enclosed pavilion called 'Anne Boleyn's Seat'. In the nineteenth century, at the end of the avenue, William Burges' church of Saint Anne was added to this sublime composition, and in the twentieth century it was declared a world heritage site by UNESCO.

The visitor centre for Fountains Abbey and Studley Royal learns from Ailsabie and applies the lessons for twentieth-century purposes. A new approach road on the axis of the Burges' spire first sees it, loses it, then sees it again, but with the obelisk in front of it.The road then goes to the visitor centre along a new axis from that obelisk. As you enter the courtyard of the building you see across it the top of the abbey tower rising out of the valley half a mile away.

You do what you will in the visitor centre, then enter a wood and lose the tower. Leaving the wood enables the discovery of a now larger, higher, apparently thinner tower; looking down over the valley edge reveals its full 160 feet. The walk along the valley edge via lookouts gradually reveals the whole vast abbey and the beginnings of the landscaped gardens. Finally, a rediscovered medieval road leads towards the layman's west front of the abbey church and into the landscaped valley itself. The visitor centre is stitched into the existing landscape and contributes a new one: it filters and enlightens the many thousands of people who wish to walk there today.

Response, Completion, Crescendo

Response

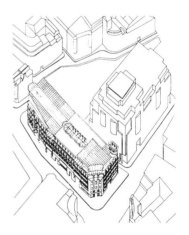

In 1994 we designed a building that spans the existing railway station, down Ludgate Hill from St Paul's and beside Ludgate Circus: and another one in the conservation area of medieval streets behind it.

The Ludgate Hill building is large in scale and makes a response to the Victorian blocks that stand beside it and opposite. It also completes the fourth segment of Ludgate Circus that was missing. The building behind it has a smaller, more detailed scale and picks up on the medieval street pattern in response to context.

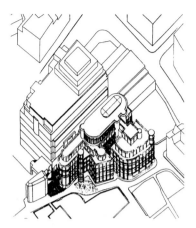
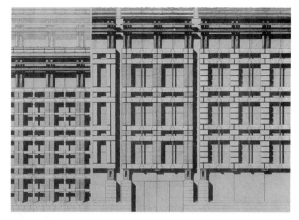

The buildings are steel framed (visibly exposed along the façades) with a loose fitting rain skin hung onto the steels. This skin is made of open-jointed Portland stone, brick, and terracotta, according to location. This modern system is composed to make radically different looking and scaled façades according to the scale of the neighbouring buildings and streets.

Completion

We made a new library for St John's College in Cambridge between 1990 and 1993.

The western side of the third court at the College is formed by an intact sixteenth-century library, complete with furniture and books. The ground floor was gradually being destroyed by attempts to interleaf modern library uses and books. This modern alteration and adaptation was also gradually and haphazardly spreading through a nineteenth-century building in Chapel Court next door. This, the Penrose Building, which contained large lecture halls, had been so chopped up and butchered over the years that its appearance was disliked. To make the Penrose Building into a modern library, the interior was cleared out to reveal its original clarity, with an entrance porch added in Chapel Court to provide accommodation above it. To complete the project, a closed apsidal building was built in the Master's Garden.

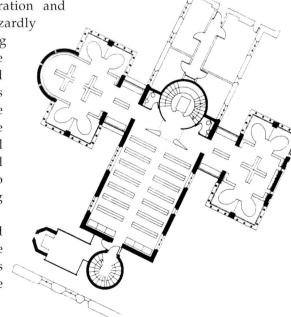

Natural ventilation and comfort were achieved by placing a lantern with reversible fan over the resulting crossing. Lanterns in the Middle Ages were to take the stinking fumes out of the middle

Figure 11.6: St John's College Library, Cambridge.

of a hall, but over the years they have become nasty little decorative objects. The Darth Vader look of the lantern is semi-deliberate.

In this library all the reading spaces are out on the edge of the building and the book shelves are in the middle, as opposed to the classic librarian's design, which is a square box, air-conditioned, me in the middle, books around the edge.

Crescendo

The Media Centre at Cheltenham was executed between 1991 and 1993.

The Art School was built in the 1960s around three courtyards on flat ground, which run in a row, north to south. Two are open, but the central yard is roofed to make an art gallery and a place of assembly. The composition is terminated by a four-storey slab at the northern end, but the ground falls steeply away to the south.

In this way it is a classic of the 1960s: the plan of Smithson's Hunstanton School overlooked by a four-storey building modelled on Saarinen's American Embassy!

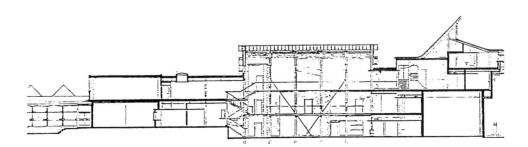

Our additions to the Art School, which houses facilities for media studies, are therefore built around a fourth, enclosed court or atrium, which steps down the hill. It has studios on either side, leading to a high crescendo at the southern end where student rooms sit above editor's offices, which in turn reside above huge film studios. Thus the existing building on the flat – designed mostly in plan – when extended, responds to the contours in both plan and section at once.

The architecture of the generation of our parents has always been unpopular, and the same can be said of the architecture of the 1960s. But we liked this 1960s building and tried to understand it and provide its diminuendo with a suitable crescendo.

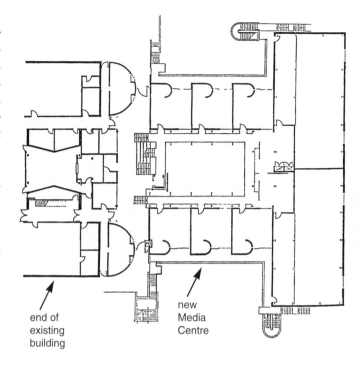

end of existing building

new Media Centre

Figure 11.7: The Media Centre, Cheltenham School of Art.

Figure 11.8: The Media Centre, Cheltenham School of Art.

Conclusion

Since Minster Lovell we have completed many buildings and schemes in 'holy' places: Oxford, Cambridge, Winchester College, Edinburgh, Barnes Village, the London green belt bordering St Paul's, Fountains Abbey and Covent Garden. All of them were agonizingly difficult to do because of the power of the lobby that would like to copy or half-copy the past by lifting features from the old buildings, or by reproducing them more or less whole. Instead, we have always tried to study and respect the formal quality of the shared places between old buildings and our new ones so that they may be enriched by the differences between the old and the new buildings that frame them. It is a hard idea to get across; pastiche is easier.

On behalf of *The Architectural Review*, Penny McGuire asked a number of architects including me if we think there is such a thing as an English tradition in architecture and, if so, whether it is a recognizable shape today. A question for the 1980s and, I assume, related to the 150th anniversary of the RIBA. My answers to the two questions are in essence: 'Yes, probably' to the first and 'No' to the second.

I want tradition in architecture to mean a shared and continuous development of the way of doing things towards practical artistic and social ends. I do not want it to mean in the estate agent's sense old-fashioned-looking housing estates and supermarkets, they are not being traditional, they are being no more than old-fashioned or nostalgic. In doing this they accurately reflect the fear of the present that many feel. The great Berthold Lubetkin told us in his Gold Medal speech that this fear was largely generated by the fact that we have discovered the means of our total destruction. Let us proceed hopefully.

Defining the cultural context of historic buildings

12

Richard MacCormac   *MacCormac Jamieson Prichard*

Summary

The universities are loyal patrons of architecture and have a tradition of commissioning new buildings from the most innovative and often radical architects of the day.

Richard MacCormac has a large oeuvre of university work, which includes many new buildings for the historic colleges of Oxford and Cambridge. His philosophy is not simply to mimic or produce a pastiche of earlier buildings on the site but to define a physical and cultural context for the building that has a relationship with the present. He uses this approach not only in historic settings but also when designing buildings that have a strong historical context such as the new library for the Ruskin archive at the University of Lancaster.

By his own admission, as an architect, he is unusual in being able to pinpoint the historical references that inform his work. His heroes in both the Classical and modern traditions of architecture include: Robert Smythson, Nicholas Hawksmoor, Sir John Vanbrugh, Sir John Soane, Alexander 'Greek' Thomson, Sir Edwin Lutyens, Frank Lloyd Wright, and more recently Sir James Stirling. However, as he points out, the heroes are 'mavericks' who took the basic tenets of Classicism to extremes in order to create great buildings.

In this chapter, Richard MacCormac describes how the understanding of historic buildings influences his designs and how, backed with the confidence of enlightened clients, he develops new designs that fit comfortably into historic contexts.

Introduction

A problem for architects at the end of the twentieth century is summed up for me when intelligent lay people ask 'Oh, are you a modern architect?' 'Well, I don't know really' I reply. The word 'modern' now has a particular historical resonance about it, because Modernism may be perceived as a development that occurred about as long ago from today as for example the Regency period was from the late Victorian. I believe that we are now in a cultural dilemma in relation to tradition and modernity. It is not just a question of *physical* context but *cultural* context, one that is always changing. This chapter addresses, from a variety of perspectives, the question of what 'history' and, implicitly, the term 'tradition' means for creative architecture today.

Robert Venturi, in his brilliant little book *Complexity and Contradiction in Architecture* was probably the first architect to see the relevance to architecture of T S Eliot's words:

> Tradition cannot be inherited and if you want it you must obtain it by great labour. It involves, in the first place, the historical sense which involves a perception not only of the pastness of the past but of its presence.[1]

Our engagement with history is essentially evaluative and, by evaluating the past and seizing upon what we find important, we are tacitly involved in a creative act. In some way we may actually change the past by attending to it, because the past does not exist, except insofar as we construct it. Therefore, I see the past and its relationship with the present as essentially dynamic. Our interventions into the past change the past and, by making those interventions in our design process, we also change the present.

The question of style

I am troubled by the question of style. The practical objection to taking an idiom from the past is that it may inhibit the technical solution to the design of a building. But there is another more subtle issue: that you limit, rather than increase, the historical allusiveness of what you are doing. This may be a paradox but John Ruskin[2] bemoaned the fact that in Dulwich most of the pubs were built in the Venetian Gothic style; then he realized that *he* was the cause, so he moved to live in the Lake District to escape 'the Frankenstein monsters of my own making.' And so it seems that Ruskin, late in life, realized that historical style was inadequate because, in its new context of time and place, it failed to deliver that to which it was supposed to allude.

This issue has become of interest to me through our design for the Ruskin Library at Lancaster University. The project, which was exhibited at the Venice

Biennale in 1996, gave me the motive to try to relate to Ruskin's perception of architecture as historical, without recourse to historical style. Ruskin saw architecture as capable of telling stories, because that is what the word 'history' really alludes to: stories about the past and what we have inherited from the past. I wanted to try to find a way of relating that Ruskinian urgency about architecture to my own inheritance, to my generation's inheritance of the idiomatic characteristics of modern architecture. In my essay, 'Architecture, memory and metaphor',[3] I wrote that metaphor is the key to 'history' because it can launch a range of allusions and gather to itself a series of ambiguous attributes that are potentially much richer than any single stylistic commitment could be. I also believe that art is often essentially metaphorical in this way; for example the artist Ian Hamilton Finlay plays a similar game by putting the familiar into an unfamiliar context. The point that I really want to make is about a way of looking at history, not stylistically, but at deeper levels of recollection and I hope to show this through the examples of projects that follow.

New buildings and historic contexts

Sainsbury Building, Worcester College, Oxford

I am very interested in Classicism and modern architecture; the Modern Movement, was profoundly affected by Classicism. One thinks of Le Corbusier and of Colin Rowe's great essay *The Mathematics of the Ideal Villa,*[4] which examines the relationship between villas by Palladio and Le Corbusier. Frank Lloyd Wright was also deeply imbued with the Classical discipline of grid organization in his buildings. This is evident in his Froebel Kindergarten Training, the key to the geometry of all his early work that has much to do with the intersections of cruciforms and squares in his plans, which is fundamental to the Classical idea of centrality.

The project at Worcester College was quite an early one in our oeuvre of university work. Set on the lake, the building is clearly idiomatically of the late twentieth century. A conventional response to Worcester College would have been a Palladian one in a literal sense because the main quadrangle of the College is Palladian in derivation, although its original conception was Hawksmoor's. The College is entered from the end of Beaumont Street where it

Figure 12.1: Worcester College, Oxford, the loggia.

presents itself as an open court that engages the street axially. On passing underneath the library one finds oneself in a wonderful loggia, which engages the breadth of the quadrangle that you are about to enter and has a lovely reflectiveness beneath it *(Figure 12.1)*. I see that loggia as a threshold between the city of Oxford and the magical garden of Worcester College.

The building frames the garden as a park, but conceals the lake, which is not revealed until you have gone further. Although the lake was formed in the early nineteenth century you experience an eighteenth-century artifice, which is not to do with architectural style but with a time sequence of disclosure: an eighteenth-century gardening device that serializes the experience of landscape. You have to go through the quadrangle out into the garden to find the lake, which is one of those serpentines that involves you in a gradual process of discovery until you finally see its end. As in an eighteenth-century park, the end of the lake might be marked by an object such as a *tempietto*, or what has just come to mind, one of my favourite places the Rievaulx Terrace, North Yorkshire where *tempietti* mark each end of a serpentine grassed walk, thus you find our building at the end of the lake at Worcester College. Here we continued an eighteenth-century idea by extending the lake around a tree, leaving the tree on an island, and then extending the water

Figure 12.2: The Sainsbury Building, Worcester College, Oxford by MacCormac Jamieson Prichard seen from across the lake.

Figure 12.3: The garden of Worcester College, Oxford seen from the Sainsbury Building.

of the lake around each side of the building so that the building initially appears to be an island *(Figure 12.2)*.

The eighteenth-century intention is that lakes are to be like rivers, so you have to find a way of ending the lake. At Worcester College the water disappears into undergrowth as though it is running away. It must also appear to have a source and, in this case, we made a series of shallow water steps, water being pumped down over them to aerate, for practical purposes, the end of the lake. Thus the building, though modern in appearance, is very much formed by its engagement with an historical landscape tradition, not with an historical style.

I have described the eighteenth-century loggia in the college as part of an entrance sequence of spaces at the end of Beaumont Street. Our building mimics the sequence, miniaturizing the notion of a loggia as a threshold between city and magical garden, framing the silhouette of trees but deferring the view of the lake. One difference is that there is a 'room' underneath the raised terrace, which takes the place of the quadrangle; through this room the water can just be seen *(Figure 12.3)*.

Fitzwilliam College, Cambridge

Shortly after completing the Worcester project we won a commission to build a new court for the relatively new Fitzwilliam College, Cambridge. Here the influence is Sir John Soane and, for various reasons, I am fascinated by his house and museum at Lincoln's Inn Fields. It is one of my favourite places, full of complex spatial illusions. The dome in the breakfast room would conventionally in a Classical building define the space but by moving the walls out from the space that the dome defines, an extraordinary ambiguity is achieved: a sense that the space might be somehow outside. I believe that Soane not only amplified spatial ideas that his mentor George Dance had initiated but perceived this amplification as latent in his collection of reconstructed Roman wall paintings. It is my theory that Soane interpreted those wall paintings into three-dimensional designs; for example, because of climate, Roman and Pompeiian houses had few windows and therefore a sense of space was achieved by intricate partial perspectives that expanded the rooms in all directions. In Soane's dining room the columns and cabinets frame niches and mirrors through which the space of the room penetrates in a Pompeiian way. He had a way of creating 'layers' of space as on the exterior of the building where he overlaid a stepped frontispiece onto the façade.

At Fitzwilliam we have taken Soane's thematic idea, breaking the elevations of the building into three layers to enable every room to have a little bay window *(Figure 12.4)*. The window is what Sir John Summerson, in his book *Heavenly Mansions* called an aedicule.[5] He developed an argument about the aedicule being derived from the miniature temple containing the god or goddess in a Classical shrine and then suggested that every window and every door is a memory of that idea, the deepest architectural memory of the idea of habitation: the little house.

Figure 12.4: Student accommodation, Fitzwilliam College, Cambridge.

Figure 12.5: Interior of student room, Fitzwilliam College, Cambridge.

Every student in this building has a little 'house', which has a roof higher than the ceiling of their room, so it appears from the inside to be a balcony that engages a space that lies, as it were, between the inside and the outside of the room *(Figure 12.5)*.

My most 'Soanian' building is the chapel for Fitzwilliam College. The historical references in this building are metaphorical and cannot easily be tied down. The design is based on a traditional church, cruciform with a longitudinal axis, but with the opportunity for centrality in the manner of Sir Christopher Wren's post-1666 churches. This device enables the chapel to intimately house a small group for Communion, or a congregation of about 150 people sitting in a conventional way facing the altar. It consists of a square structure inside a round structure. The square structure is part of a longitudinal axis that projects the dynamic of the existing terrace by Sir Denys Lasdun, for which this building is a kind of end-piece.

Within the circular space and the square frame of the building is suspended a 'vessel' of wood, an idea that probably came to me after seeing the Vassar ship in Stockholm and the Viking ships in the Oslo Viking Ship Museum. At the time it did not occur to me how potent the ship is as a symbol in world religion; it symbolizes the right of passage, redemption, the journey of life, and the after-life represented by the burial ship.

Inside the entrance to the chapel is a crypt above which the 'vessel' is suspended.[6] To enter the the vessel you climb stairs, which ascend around each side. This staircase was probably influenced by Asplund's City Library in Stockholm but when I am working on new ideas I am not consciously aware of thinking, 'Oh, Asplund's staircases in Stockholm Library would be the thing to do.' Architects carry a great deal of historical 'baggage' around with them, a largely sub-conscious database that needs to be accessed just at the right time.

Figure 12.6: The tree on the axis of the east window from the chapel of Fitzwilliam College, Cambridge.

The cubic frame that supports the roof is precast concrete, which is polished like marble thus proving what marvellous things can be done with concrete. Between the square and the circle the roof is a timber fan – geometrically part of a cone that is glazed around the edge – a trick that Soane used in his breakfast room, letting light in at the perimeter, creating an ambiguous, very gentle space. The client was unsure about the positioning of the staircase that links the crypt to the congregational space and allows performers and the chaplain their own access but, in addition to being useful, it disengages the east window. The tree outside, coincidentally, happens to be exactly on the same axis, and that too is a potent symbol *(Figure 12.6)*.

Wadham College, Oxford

I go through fads of enthusiasm for certain buildings or architects. For me the most interesting architects of Classicism in England are what I call 'maverick' Classicists, amongst whom I include Robert Smythson at the end of the sixteenth century, Hawksmoor and Vanbrugh at the end of the seventeenth century, Soane at the end of the eighteenth century, Alexander 'Greek' Thomson in the nineteenth century, and Lutyens and possibly James Stirling in the twentieth century.

The geometry of Robert Smythson's Hardwick Hall (1590-97) with its fierce self-confidence, modernity and ignorance is unprecedented; it belongs to a time of ingenuity. In Mark Girouard's book on Robert Smythson there are two poems: one by Sir Walter Raleigh, an exquisitely sensuous love poem that can be read either vertically or horizontally, and a typical Elizabethan poem, which plays geometric games.

Hir face	*Hir tong*	*Hir wit*
So faire	*So sweete*	*So sharpe*
First bent	*Then drew*	*Then hit*
Mine eie	*Mine eare*	*My heart*
Mine eie	*Mine eare*	*My heart*
To like	*To learne*	*To love*
Her face	*Hir tong*	*Her wit*
Doth lead	*Doth teach*	*Doth move*
Oh face	*Oh tong*	*Oh wit*
With frownes	*With cheeke*	*With smarte*
Wrong not	*Vex not*	*Wound not*
Mine eie	*Mine eare*	*My heart*
Mine eie	*Mine eare*	*My heart*
To learne	*To knowe*	*To feare*
Hir face	*Hir tong*	*Hir wet*
Doth lead	*Doth teach*	*Doth sweare*[7]

I like these ideas because in all creative processes there are various interpretations on offer with a variety of layers of meaning, which is true of science as it is of art. In the plan of Hardwick there is a geometry that establishes a cross or double cross intersecting the great rectangular volume in the centre of the building.

At Wadham College, the Classical centre piece of the seventeenth-century quadrangle is attached iconically onto the vernacular to make an allusion, which is very much what Post-Modernism has been about in the twentieth century. It is entirely different from the way that Smythson deployed his proto-Classicism at Hardwick, which was integral. In our design we had to achieve a very high density to fit 84 student rooms onto a very small site; it has a residential density about three times that of 1960s tower blocks – approximately 300 students to the acre. The key to our design is very much in the idiom of Hardwick Hall with its arrangement of pavilions and terraces.

Figure 12.7: Student accommodation, Wadham College, Oxford.

There is a body of accommodation at the rear of the building with pavilions at the front that allow daylight and sunlight to penetrate and to give views out from this deeply developed site. It takes the idea from Hardwick of prospect towers and develops further the hybrid architecture of brick and precast concrete that we used at Fitzwilliam, Cambridge. The prospect towers engage the splendid skyline of spires and cupolas in Oxford above the general roofline – these wonderful objects pop up dramatically. The street running through the scheme is only 2.4m wide so cills are used to reflect light into the rooms. I must admit that the tower of New College Chapel that is framed in the view was unexpected; it came as a complete surprise when the scaffolding was struck, which goes to prove that sometimes architects are lucky *(Figure 12.7)*.

St John's College, Oxford

Following the project at Wadham we developed a much more complex kind of 'Hardwick' for St John's College adjacent to the Thomas White quadrangle, which was designed by Arup Associates in the early 1970s – a building that I very much admire. Our building, which is called the Garden Quadrangle, is probably the most 'Classical' building that I have designed. It is not a Classicism of the Orders in any conventional sense but more to do with a site that was rather mysterious and unknown to the College in the sense that they were leasing out some laboratory buildings there. I felt that the mystery of the site should be maintained in the idea of a cavernous underworld.

I was stimulated by Tom Marcus[8] to speculate whether Piranesi must have perceived in the discovery of Pompeii the idea that underworlds, through which you look up at the real world, are in some sense more real than the temporal world that is outside them. There is an interesting duality here. An example of a mysterious underworld can be seen in Alexander Pope's grotto at Twickenham and its opposite in the beautiful drawing by Sir John Vanbrugh of a cemetery, rather like the island of *San Michele* in Venice where all the obelisks and cypress trees are packed together and contained by a tight retaining wall *(Figure 12.8)*. An analogy

Figure 12.8: San Michele, Venice. Drawing by Sir John Vanbrugh.

with this in modern architecture, quite different of course, are Utzon's courthouses in northern Denmark where the natural landscape flows like a sea around little brick court houses with garden courts bursting with shrubs and trees. They are like bouquets of architecture bursting out of a natural landscape. Such images helped generate the design of the upper part of the building.

At St John's College the image of Soane's Bank of England is important; it is a gigantic top-lit underworld *(Figure 12.9)*. The model of the building shows three circular top-lit spaces with pendentives, which are Soanian in construction; two are roofed and one has no roof. There are very few clients who will allow you to build a room without a roof. As well as working with enlightened clients I also enjoy employing artists to work outside their own experience. The building is approached through a gate designed by the jewellery designer Wendy Ramshaw who, using her jeweller's imagination, set a double lens into the gate, which creates an 'Alice in Wonderland' effect as you look through it; the whole building can be seen momentarily from only four feet away. Another artist, Alex Beleschenko, designed and made the glass screens around the courtyard, which undoubtedly are a masterwork *(Figure 12.10)*.

A Classical characteristic of this building is that it has a base, its underworld, above which is a formal garden that continues the context of the college onto a high level and is surrounded by towers, which address

Figure 12.9: The Garden Quadrangle, St John's College, Oxford.

Figure 12.10: Glass screens around the courtyard of St John's College, Oxford by Alex Beleschenko.

you like Michelangelo's Capitol buildings in Rome – you look at them and they look back at you – they are anthropomorphic. I wanted these towers to look out, to address the garden and the visitor as well as offering views. The domes of the building are painted with frescoes, painted by Fleur Kelly, which are possibly the largest that have been painted in the second half of this century in England. The building is largely constructed of precast concrete, which has been weathered in a manner that takes its cue largely from Classical detailing.

The Ruskin Library, Lancaster University

Finally, I return to the Ruskin Library at Lancaster University, which gave me an interest in the idea of architectural narrative: what architecture could say to you. The full story is in my essay for the Venice Biennale[9] but the idea is that the building is like a keep within which is another keep, the archive, a Venetian red cabinet 18m long and three storeys high. It just happens that this metaphor has turned out to be extremely efficient in conservation terms. This will be the first major archive to be built without air conditioning because of the stability gained from the combination of the two massive 'keeps' and the volume of air between them.

With its oak frame and bronze fixings the archive is like a huge treasure chest or, alternatively, it can be interpreted as the choir of a cathedral with the reading room at the far end of the building being the sanctuary. Ruskin called St Mark's

Figure 12.11: Ruskin Library, University of Lancaster.

Cathedral, Venice 'a vast illuminated missal';[10] the archive in the Ruskin Library symbolizes that too, and stands as the corpus of Ruskin's work. The floor as you enter the building is made of glass and slate and you can look down through it. Ruskin used to dream of looking at the waters of Venice and seeing the horses of St Mark's being harnessed under water. The glass and slate floor, which is under-lit, is like the lagoon or the canals of Venice, with the Venetian red archive emerging through it like an island.

At one end of the archive, behind doors, is an image of the north-west portal of St Mark's. This image is one we found in a book of Ruskin's daguerreotypes,[13] which are images on metal that Ruskin might have termed 'fugitive' because you can only vaguely make out the picture. Using computer technology, the artist Alex Beleschenko digitized a photograph of the daguerreotype and expanded it from about 200 millimetres to four metres high. Glassmakers in Germany, using a technique for putting platinum into etched glass, have produced a ghostly image that has been placed behind the doors. The idea of that image is to try to capture a memory of the past in a very fragile Proustian way.

Conclusion

This chapter has discussed architecture in a particular way. The purpose and functional efficiency of the buildings has been assumed so as to address the significance that architecture can gain from its historical context, in both a physical and cultural sense.

It has to be said that the exigencies of the modern world, the preoccupation with cost and accountability and dwindling public funds do not tend to encourage the approach that I have described. It takes far sighted , aspirational and enlightened clients to see how far architecture can venture beyond the crude agenda of cost and quantity. All the projects described have relied on such clients.

Part of the original polemic of Modernism was to wipe clean the slate of architectural history. As a consequence, architecture lost a whole discourse of recollected meanings and restricted itself to functional and technical explanations. Architecture conceived in an historical context brings with it the potential for recovering the discourse that Modernism dismantled.

Notes and references

1 ELIOT T S, *Tradition and the Individual Talent,* 1919 quoted in VENTURI R, *Complexity and Contradiction in Architecture*, Architectural Press, 1977.
2 RUSKIN J, *The Pall Mall Gazette,* 1872.
3 MacCORMAC R, 'Architecture, memory and metaphor', essay for the Venice Biennale, 1996.
4 ROWE C, *The Mathematics of the Ideal Villa,* Cambridge, Mass., MIT Press, 1976.
5 SUMMERSON J, *Heavenly Mansions and other essays on architecture*, Cresset Press, 1949.
6 The contractors Johnson and Bailey of Cambridge used 7,800 screws to fasten the planks onto the frame. Whilst they were making the mock-up they realized that the screws could not be pelleted as the planks would be too thin if they were to be flexible enough to bend round the minimum radius – what should they do? 'Well,' I said, 'go out and get 7,800 stainless steel screws and grit blast them individually.' They knew that was a joke but what they did achieve was to line up the slot in every screw east west, amazing!
7 GIROUARD M, *Robert Smythson and the architecture of the Elizabethan era,* Country Life, 1996.
8 MARCUS T, *Buildings and Power*, Routledge, 1993.
9 MacCORMAC, *op. cit.*
10 RUSKIN J, *The Stones of Venice,* vol I, ch.4, paragraph 46.

The essential elements in developing new designs for historic settings

13

Spencer de Grey *Foster and Partners*

Summary

Foster and Partners are renowned for their contemporary architectural designs but they are not normally associated with historic settings. However, since their highly successful project for the Sackler Galleries at the Royal Academy of Arts, they have established a reputation for the treatment of historical buildings in both Britain and Continental Europe.

In this chapter, Spencer de Grey discusses three projects from the practice that all have required different approaches because of their very special historic contexts. At the Royal Academy of Arts, London, there was the problem of how to regenerate the heart of the Academy by knitting together two separate parts of the building, built in different centuries, to form the new Sackler Galleries. In Nîmes, the new Cultural Centre explores the insertion of a major new building into a sensitive, historic context. At the British Museum in London, where the project is still underway, there is an exciting opportunity to expose the exterior of the historic Reading Room, which has been hidden from public view for years and use this as the central focus of a new public space linked to an urban scheme stretching from St Pancras in the north down to the river.

As he explains, the process requires not only inspiration but a careful methodology from the initial stages of the project to realization. He stresses the importance of teamwork, an enlightened client and above all, the need for a 'champion' who will steer the project through the complex stages to the final realization of the building.

Introduction

When approached to make this contribution, I was asked, 'Does your inspiration for buildings come as a sudden flash or is it a careful, methodical, scientific, step-by-step process?' Obviously, inspiration plays a very high part in any architect's design but as I will show, there is also great importance attached to looking at all the options, and through a step-by-step process, challenging one idea against another. This methodology is particularly relevant when working in an historic context.

All of the projects discussed involve historic buildings where the existing fabric has been a major consideration in the design. The inspiration for our designs gradually evolves through a careful process that involves looking at the historical background, considering the details of the existing fabric and then making decisions about the layers of history. All of this has to be matched against the needs of the building and its context.

This process takes place in close consultation with members of the project team and in particular, the client. In our experience, all successful projects need the stamp of an individual. It may be that that individual works through committees but there has to be a project sponsor within the client dedicated to the project. No matter how the project is organized, whatever the complexities, you need a 'champion'. This is crucially important, particularly working with complex projects in existing buildings and especially where the project is breaking new ground, which all projects should do in some way or another.

Sackler Galleries, Royal Academy of Arts, London

This was a very important project for the practice, particularly as it was really the first time we had worked in an historic context; and the Royal Academy, with its extraordinary array of architectural and artistic talent, was a rather challenging client. As the lead architects on this project we had an important role to play in channelling specialist involvement and keeping control over the total design. We worked very closely from the very beginning with quite a large team including Julian Harrap who advised on the restoration of the fabric; English Heritage, and the City of Westminster Planning Department.

Figure 13.1: The Royal Academy of Arts, Piccadilly, London.

Figures 13.2 & 13.3: The Sackler Galleries showing the light well (above) where the new lift hallway now stands (below).

The Royal Academy building was originally designed by Hugh May in the seventeenth century, with a façade on Piccadilly that was transformed by Lord Burlington and William Kent in the mid-eighteenth century. When the Royal Academy moved there in the 1860s, the Victorians not only added the main galleries on the site of the garden to the rear but also added a substantial floor on top of Burlington House itself. This additional floor became the Diploma Galleries, a small suite of galleries for the display of diploma works of the members of the Royal Academy and the Schools. These galleries were to be the centre-piece of our work when the Royal Academy approached Sir Norman Foster, himself a member of the Academy, to look at possibilities for environmental improvement within the galleries, which were far too hot in summer and with far too much light to meet the demanding criteria for loan exhibitions. The galleries were a wasted opportunity resulting in the handsome rooms on the *piano nobile* having to be transformed on an *ad hoc* basis for smaller, travelling exhibitions. They were expensive to run and rather an unsuitable setting for such exhibitions.

As the project progressed, it became more complicated than simply looking at the environmental conditions of three Victorian rooms on the upper floors of the building. The whole question of access needed to be addressed: how to move both people and exhibits up to the galleries together with the wider implications of creating this new exhibition suite in relation to the whole building.

When the Victorians built the main galleries to the rear of the Royal Academy, they had the good sense to separate the new construction from the original house by a gap of about three or four metres; it was this gap that became the clue to the whole project. Over the years, this space had become a rather 'tacky' light-well with

Figures 13.4: The Sackler Galleries, stairwell to and from the galleries.

Figures 13.5: The lift hallway showing the coping stones used for the display of sculpture.

very unloved twentieth-century additions including lavatories for the public. This neglected space became the centre of the design. The main galleries had been built directly behind the garden façade, which was the subject of remodelling at the beginning of the nineteenth century.

An important consideration was the balance between creation and re-creation – how did the two elements of the building relate when, having stripped everything away, we came to put into that space a new lift, new staircases and new floors at the upper level. Should it be a totally pastiche re-creation of the original façade or should what had happened in the intervening period be respected and revealed in the approach to the design? Should the new insertion be a copy, an imitation of an historic style, or should it be of today, reflecting the transformation that the Academy had, over the years, undergone.

We adopted an approach where the new insertion was very much of today, very much in the language of our practice. When considering the historic elements of the project, we decided not to re-create an exact copy of the garden façade. The situation was now very different – it had become an internal space, no longer outside, with new floors at various levels. Although the historic façade is visible, its setting is very different from the original. We adopted a strategy of using original materials and re-creating the geometry of that original façade but not trying to create an exact copy.

There was a large area where a 1950s metal window had been inserted and a great deal of re-working had to be done. Some of the plasterwork is original; the new work – much smoother in its finish – is clearly differentiated. The new stairs and lift lead to the new reception for the main galleries. Here we removed the lead from the coping stones at the top of the Victorian main galleries and used the coping stone for the display of sculpture. The new galleries respect the geometry of the original space. We maintained the layout and configuration of the original three rooms but transformed the quality of natural light and introduced sophisticated air-conditioning. These requirements were very important parts of the brief that lead to a new vaulted roof, which replaced a rather heavy Victorian gilded ceiling.

Our solution transformed a part of the building where nothing but decay existed and has created a new heart to the Royal Academy, providing a suite of small galleries that is recognized as one of the best in the world. The Academy was very pleased with it and, although the process was rather complex, it was worth all the effort. Although the project was quite small in cost and scale, it was a pioneering scheme that has spawned a whole range of other projects. It was the first time we had made a major intervention into a listed historic building. It showed that contemporary design can be combined with the regeneration of historic fabric in a sympathetic way. Museums and the cultural world in general, now have the confidence to be bolder in their approach. Many of the current Lottery and Millennium projects are making major interventions into listed buildings; it is not without interest that many museums in London are undergoing modern interventions, including our own project at the British Museum, the Wallace Collection, Somerset House and the Museum of Modern Art at Bankside.

Cultural Centre, Nîmes

This project was the result of an international competition for a new cultural centre in the city of Nîmes. The city had suffered under thirty years of local Communist rule from the 1950s through to the 1980s, by which time it had become run down. The new mayor very much wanted to change that pattern and to inject new life to give a sense of identity, a sense of place, a social focus, a new heart to Nîmes. In France, mayors hold much more than an honorary position; they are politicians with considerable political influence. This project formed part of the new mayor's political agenda.

Nîmes is not a large city but very important in terms of its historic monuments, particularly the great Roman Amphitheatre and the Maison Carrée – the most

Figure 13.6: The Maison Carrée at Nîmes with the remains of the Neo-Classical façade of the Opera House at the head of the square.

perfect example of a small Roman Temple in existence. This great historic monument was sitting in its square with some quite good provincial domestic architecture surrounding it but the whole area was run down. It was an unloved space, dominated by roads and car parking. At the head of the square stood a Neo-Classical façade, the only remains of the Opera House that was burned down in the 1950s. Here was a typical urban problem that many cities suffer from today.

During the first visits to the site we carried out a good deal of analysis to understand the key elements of the city – the major buildings and the road structure. There is a very important diagonal route that leads from the centre to the other key historic feature, *Les Jardins de la Fontaine*, the great water gardens on the outskirts of the city. The site of the new Centre is therefore at an important junction, not only with the axis of the Maison Carrée but also with the diagonal route. This understanding, or analysis of the city, was an important influence on the design development of the project.

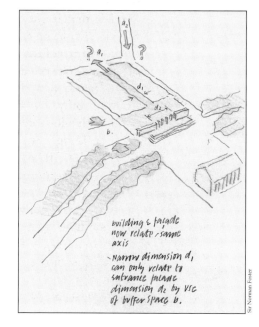

Figure 13.7: Sketch diagram of the site by Sir Norman Foster showing relationships of space.

A major consideration was what should happen to the historic colonnade of the Opera House on the site of the new Cultural Centre. Only the colonnade remained but should that be kept or should it be removed; what were the implications of that strategy? In the early days of the commission there was heated debate about the retention of the colonnade. In considering the regeneration of this city centre, should the major new building be hidden behind the historic colonnade or should its presence be felt on that important street front and on the whole of the square? Should it be visible and should it regenerate new life? After a considerable number of studies, the decision was taken with the mayor and the people of Nîmes that the colonnade, the last vestige of the Opera House, should be taken down and the new building revealed. With the help of a series of models showing alternative designs, both keeping the portico and removing it, the mayor was convinced that, if he wanted to make a strong statement and rejuvenate a run-down square, albeit housing the Maison Carrée, then the right solution was to be bold. It would have been a much weaker solution if the Classical portico had been retained.

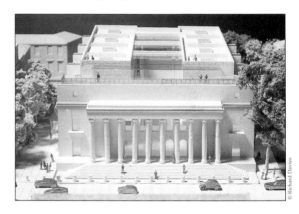

We felt that it was very important that there should be a definition of the entrance portico of the new building to relate to the Maison Carrée itself. The first idea was a very simple colonnade supported only by columns at the corners, with a louvered screen in front of the building. But the scale was monumental in relation to the quite delicate, small scale of the temple. So that began to lead to a solution with a more structured, colonnaded portico, with a stronger vertical emphasis to break down the scale. This related more closely to the colonnade of the temple itself. In the final design there is a

Figures 13.8 & 13.9: A series of models showing alternative designs, both keeping the portico and removing it.

strong vertical emphasis of the columns in the portico. Thus, you move through the portico up a short flight of stairs to the main entrance. From the heart of the building you can cross to a secondary entrance on the diagonal at the far corner of the building, leading you onto the water gardens.

Looking at the building in section, the height is a crucial issue in the whole development of the design. The upper two floors are gallery spaces, one for temporary exhibitions, one for the permanent collection. The principle entrance and shop is at ground level. On the lower levels below ground is the library with both the books, CDs and so on. At the heart of the building is a great staircase, sitting in a rectangular space with generous natural light from above – a courtyard. Courtyards are very common in Nîmes; they are a feature of the local architecture. With the accommodation wrapping around on four sides there was an opportunity to create such a courtyard, albeit enclosed with the staircase in it linking all levels. Studies were carried out on whether that courtyard should be permanently enclosed or whether in fact it should be openable. We looked at the options for having sliding roofs so that in summer that space could be opened up. Eventually, the decision was taken to keep it as a permanently enclosed space with plenty of natural light from above.

When looking at the overall plan, the relationship of the new building to the Maison Carrée is obviously a crucial factor but the impact on the whole area needed to be considered. Working with the mayor, we looked at the setting of the new building and the setting of the Maison Carrée, with a view to providing a more unified total approach to the landscaping of the whole of the square and surrounding streets. The project gradually grew in importance, eventually becoming a major urban project for the heart of Nîmes.

Figure 13.10: The Cultural Centre, which has generated a new social focus for the city of Nîmes.

The road running through the square had to remain but there was the opportunity of repaving the whole of the square and uniting the centre with the surrounding buildings. This provided an opportunity to simplify the setting of the Roman Temple, of developing paving patterns and configurations that were rooted in original Roman paving patterns. Local stone was used as part of that strategy to provide a more handsome, more integrated setting for both the new building and the existing one. Car parking was removed and pedestrian space was created to allow stronger interaction between the buildings around the square. One important issue, crucial in any urban design, was the appearance of the buildings at night. Working with Claude Engle, the distinguished American lighting consultant, we developed very discreet floodlighting, recessed within the paving.

Figure 13.11: Lighting designed by Claude Engle.

The life of the area was totally transformed. The once neglected square has now become a popular venue, with many cafes. There is an extraordinary sense of coming together with the new building generating a new social focus for both everyone who lives there and visitors to the city.

Figure 13.12: The British Museum, London.

The British Museum

The project at the British Museum is highly relevant in terms of the treatment of buildings in an historic context. The Museum is one of the most visited museums in the world, with over six million visitors a year. It has an extraordinary collection of galleries but it is very short of general circulation space. In fact, the galleries become almost intolerable at peak times and those peak moments run all through the year. The Museum is not only congested but the circulation patterns are very convoluted, which makes it difficult to find your way. There are so many people in the galleries that it makes it almost impossible to see and enjoy the extraordinary exhibits.

The building has a central courtyard, rarely seen by anyone today, as you now pass through enclosed corridors to get into the circular Reading Room at the heart

Figure 13.13: Photomontage of the British Museum, showing the concept of the new central court.

of the courtyard. The courtyard originally contained a very handsome garden where people could walk, relax and get a breath of fresh air. It was the main lung of the Museum but it only lasted for about two years from 1852 to 1854. In 1854, Robert Smirke's brother, Sydney, began the construction of the Reading Room and it was at that point that the great courtyard was lost as a public focus for the Museum. In time, the Reading Room grew ancillary buildings for the storage of more books. These additions were destroyed in the Second World War and subsequently rebuilt.

The recent move of the British Library to St Pancras has freed about forty per cent of the space in the Museum. This includes the area in the courtyard – the Reading Room itself – the King's Library and quite a large amount of area to the north. It has provided an opportunity not only to provide more space for the Museum but to transform radically the circulation patterns within the Museum. There is an opportunity to take down the 1950s buildings around the drum of the

Figure 13.14: CAD image of the central court at the British Museum.

Reading Room to recreate one of the great courtyards in London. The courtyard can be enclosed with a glass roof and a new floor introduced at the principal level. This will become the focal point of the museum and take the pressure off the galleries, to allow visitors more space to circulate.

Looking at the cross-section of the building, a new floor is to be inserted at the same level as the Reading Room. The space will be enclosed with a lightweight steel and glass roof. Beneath that main level there will be a new education centre and new galleries for the ethnographic collection, which will be brought back from Burlington Gardens. At the heart of the space, the Reading Room will be restored as a major library and information centre for the Museum. It is proposed that the outside of the Reading Room, only partly clad today, will be re-clad in stone so that it becomes an integral part of the total courtyard.

This project concerns more than a public courtyard at the heart of the Museum. There is an opportunity to remove all the car parking in the Forecourt at the front and to upgrade the quality of the formal landscape. This will enable a public route to run right through the Museum, linking the University area to the north through Montague Place down Museum Street to Covent Garden. This heritage route could then link the new British Library at St Pancras, the new Channel Tunnel terminal and Kings Cross through Bloomsbury to the Great Court and then down to Covent Garden. With the new Hungerford Bridge, it will then be possible to link that route across to the South Bank. This is a project that we are currently working on with both English Heritage, Camden and Westminster Councils. However, as with most urban planning projects, miracles are not achieved overnight.

Figure 13.15: CAD image of the central court.

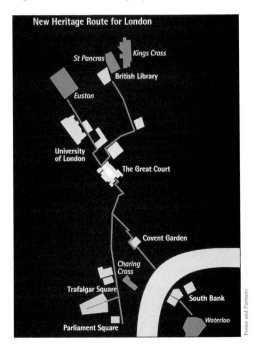

Figure 13.16: New Heritage route for London.

Pulling teeth and filling cavities!

14

John Lyall *John Lyall architects*

Summary

Regeneration in urban areas frequently involves listed buildings and conservation areas where redevelopment requires a delicate balance between protection of the historic fabric and the creation of up-to-date facilities for new uses.

John Lyall, who has in the past been involved in several projects concerning both the regeneration of historic buildings and wide open industrial areas, describes two recent projects in historic urban areas. The first is Kirkgate, Leeds, which was in medieval times the 'High Street' of the settlement but more recently has suffered neglect with the shift of the commercial centre of the city further north, away from the railway and the river. Here, the fragments of the historic fabric are being knitted together with brand new buildings through an architectural process that he likens to dentistry.

The second project is St Anne's Wharf, Norwich, which like Kirkgate in Leeds has suffered from neglect with the decline of trade and industry in that area and a city-wide change towards white-collar employment. Here a similar approach has been adopted although a far greater amount of demolition and new building has been necessary.

In both cases a philosophy of consolidating the old and celebrating the new has been adopted, which provides a clear distinction between the historic remains and the new buildings. The aim is to revitalize historic urban areas by making buildings that can be adapted to new uses and maintain a contribution to a constantly evolving urban pattern.

Introduction

For me as an architect there are two sides to urban regeneration that frequently elicit a different design response. They are often very distinct, depending on location, and can stimulate ideas for new architecture from the richness, or even poverty, of their physical characteristics.

The first category covers sites usually described as 'urban wastelands': derelict industrial land often devoid of any real context because any buildings that were once on the site have been demolished. However, what sometimes remain are large fragments of infrastructure such as docks, canals, railway sidings, cranes etc. To design buildings for totally new uses in these locations can be an exhilarating experience because the first new designs can not only act as a catalyst for further inspired development but they can also assume a courageous freedom of expression in the surroundings. The new buildings have a responsibility to establish the level of design quality for the many that will follow. Therefore, there is a good argument for only the most talented and innovative architects and urbanists to be let loose on the newly-cleared territory in order to set the tone. Most design-conscious local authorities and development corporations know that this is more easily said than done but they should never cease to strive for quality.

The second type of site is more common and often smaller. It is typically within a busy, urban centre and frequently contains strong physical remnants of an historical past that, mercifully, has been overlooked during large-scale redevelopment that occurred during the 1960s or 1970s. The buildings, often dirty and decaying, are frequently in parts of town synonymous with drugs, alcohol and prostitution. Regeneration as a cleansing act does not solve these problems, which move on elsewhere. However, there is often sufficient historical fabric to be both restored and reinvented for new uses. A great deal of thought then has to be put into the new buildings that will sit alongside the historic remnants and intermesh to create the re-considered urban pattern.

I have become accustomed to making a mark with a new building in wide-open industrially derelict areas (for example Cardiff Bay and Tottenham Hale) where, because there is no historical precedent, there is opportunity for a greater freedom of expression. The sites with more remaining 'physical' history are more of a challenge for the architect. The responsibility feels greater, if only because there are many interested and opinionated 'experts' waiting in the wings to give the site a hot climate of scrutiny – something to which it had never been subjected until an enthusiastic architect came along with new ideas. Planners, conservationists, consultees and civic societies all have their own views and visions of what they feel is the correct solution for the physical regeneration of our client's site. Not surprisingly, these visions often hark back to what would be considered a charmingly authentic remodelling of the architecture that, according to records, existed 100 to 150 years ago. This viewpoint is at last becoming less prevalent, largely due to the fact that even the most sensitive commercial developers cannot fund a scheme unless it offers space and accessibility, with better facilities than otherwise available in the tight urban grain that grew by accident over the centuries. Therefore, a degree of balance is required in the approach to a design to bring out the best in the historic context whilst integrating uncompromising modern architecture that is not purely a stylistic device but will stand the test of time and record the age in which we live.

I have selected two current examples of urban regeneration from our practice to illustrate my views. The first is in the Kirkgate area of Leeds, and the second in Norwich covering the land between King Street and the River Wensum. Both are conservation areas, containing some important listed buildings, and both have a recent history of industrial or commercial decline.

Kirkgate, Leeds

My design philosophy for the re-development of the Kirkgate site takes its lead, to a certain extent, from the manner in which I adapted two nearby listed buildings in Leeds – the Corn Exchange and the Third White Cloth Hall. These fine buildings were given a new lease of life as shops and restaurants for the same enlightened client, David Houghton of Speciality Shops plc. The approach to the Third White Cloth Hall, which dates from 1760, was to consolidate the fragile historic remains (both Georgian and Victorian) and to simply expose and celebrate our designs for the new, modern steel supporting structure, glazing and atrium. In this way there is a clear distinction between the original fabric, and the new intervention. As an

Figures 14.1 & 14.2: Third White Cloth Hall, Leeds.

architectural practice, it is not within our vocabulary to attempt a pastiche of an original style with new elements added. There is a lack of integrity about such an approach that would confuse the understanding of the building's history in years to come. I also believe that all our work should reflect the design aspirations and technology of our age. Why on earth should we go backwards?

The rejuvenation of the Corn Exchange and the Third White Cloth Hall was a great act of faith for our developer client, David Houghton: faith that the people of Leeds would wish to colonize and enjoy this derelict part of Leeds again. His acquisition of more derelict property in Crown Street, Call Lane and Kirkgate, is testimony to his recognition that a greater 'critical mass' of regeneration was necessary to support the investment in the first two completed buildings.

Historical maps indicate how Leeds grew up in medieval times on the banks of the River Aire; Kirkgate was the important 'High Street' of that settlement leading down to the church. Subsequent expansion shifted the centre of the city further northwards as the centuries passed so, by the twentieth century, the most important business and retail areas flourished in Briggate and the streets around the Headrow and Vicar Lane. Whilst the middle of this century saw a gradual decline in the property between Kirkgate and the river, the impressive Kirkgate Market mercifully seems to have maintained its attractions over the years. Along with the usual reasons for defunct industries moving out of the city centre and with no reason for the River Aire to be navigated for trade, warehouses, factories and small commercial buildings became redundant in a city that seemed to be concentrating its efforts on its commercial interests elsewhere. This small, traditional part of town was left to rot because no-one could think of a new role for it to play. The saving grace was that this lack of care and attention protected the area from the complete rape and pillage that occurred elsewhere in the centre of Leeds in the 1960s and 1970s under the banner of 'comprehensive redevelopment'. I refer, of course, to the massive shopping centres and office blocks interlinked by high-level concrete walkways that are now trying to reinvent themselves because of the resurgence of interest in the traditional shopping areas. Amongst the neglect and shabbiness remained some fine buildings (in need of urgent attention) and an urban scale that seemed a more appropriate guide for future development.

By the early 1980s, although the people of Leeds would come to the city centre to shop in the daytime, its pulling power for night-time entertainment seemed to be in decline. At that time the popular restaurants were on the outskirts of of the city and there was little of quality in the centre.

Our work in the 1980s on the Corn Exchange and Third White Cloth Hall led me to investigate old maps and archives so, when we started considering the regeneration of Kirkgate, these historical sources were crucial to the understanding of the fabric that we had inherited for our work. We were able to trace how the urban pattern had developed over the seventeenth, eighteenth and nineteenth centuries as an ever-changing system of main routes, networks of alleys (or

Figure 14.3: Crown Court, Leeds, showing the area of new development, adjacent to the distinctive form of the refurbished Corn Exchange.

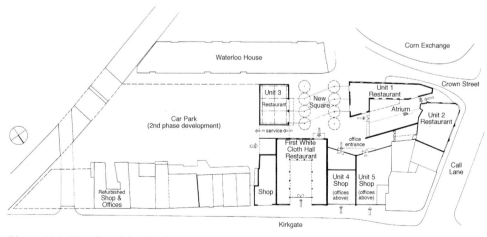

Figure 14.4: Site plan of the development area.

ginnels), and the occasional prominent building. The orthogonal lines between Kirkgate and the Calls were most radically altered by the Victorian railway engineers who forged a huge viaduct diagonally across to make a connection to York. This must have had a devastating effect on the life and trade of the area, which was effectively cut in two. As a consequence the grand rectangular courtyard of the Third White Cloth Hall was sliced up and it is perhaps remarkable that at least the front entrance remains to this day.

In studying what was left of the buildings between Kirkgate and Crown Street, it occurred to me that our urban regeneration work is rather like dentistry. The task is to bring out the best in remaining good quality structures, to remove buildings that are decaying or ugly, and to replace them with new architecture of an appropriate scale. This new architecture should not attempt an historic pastiche but should be firmly of our age in the late twentieth century, using modern technology and fulfilling current commercial requirements.

Our main scheme for this area was anchored by two new buildings at opposite ends of Kirkgate, sitting like bookends in the place of soon-to-be-demolished structures. Between them a whole cocktail of old terraced buildings of different vintages are to receive a facelift. In each of these units the fenestration, shopfronts and roofs are different, as are the upper floor levels, which give few real clues or reference points to the new infill. However, a dimensional analysis of the façades revealed an approximate horizontal module of six metres and we continued this rhythm in the new buildings. We then deliberately played with an almost random fenestration pattern to echo the lively anarchy of the old elevations. In the new elevations red bricks are to be used to match existing brickwork but the new bricks are to be stack-bonded in panels, edged by grey steel angle frames. In certain blank sections of wall, azure blue glass mosaic is to be used to work with the pale green verdigris of the copper roofs. The roofs are curved, linear vaulted spaces supported by glulam timbers and lined internally with ply-wood for a 'studio-office' environment.

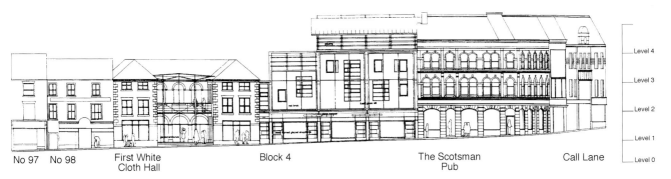

Figure 14.5: Elevation to Kirkgate, Leeds.

Figure 14.6: Perspective view of units 4 and 5,   Figure 14.7: Courtyard view of the White Cloth
Kirkgate.   Hall.

Like the Third White Cloth Hall, the even older remains of the First White Cloth
Hall are restored and supported using similar modern steelwork technology. The
central rectangular courtyard is covered by a glass roof using Planar glazing to
create a minimum intervention; this new roof and glass façade is supported by four
slim steel columns.

Historic urban areas present special financial problems too; quality regeneration
does not come cheap. While the Corn exchange transformation was achieved by the
developer without grants, the Third White Cloth Hall and the Kirkgate project have
only been possible with public sector financial support added to the private
developer commitment. This grant negotiation process, together with the recent
economic recession, has inevitably slowed up the work on the ground, which is
now developing on a building by building basis. There is never a 'quick fix'
solution to urban regeneration; anyone committed to the process has to be prepared
for long-term involvement. You learn not by theory but by doing it; great things can
be achieved but you have to be patient and a realist. Your ideas will not happen
until both the market and the community are ready for them.

St Anne's Wharf, Norwich

In medieval times Norwich was the second most important city in England, with
industries based on its agricultural surroundings (brewing, woollen cloth, leather
goods and milling) and river connections to the sea, which made convenient access

Figure 14.8: St Anne's Wharf, Norwich. Model of development area.

to Holland with whom it did a great deal of trade. For centuries, the banks of the River Wensum housed the mills, warehouses and wharfs that served the lively economy of East Anglia. Lanes ran from the river to join King Street, which was always an important central artery of the city.

Now, sadly, the industry has virtually disappeared and King Street is an unloved, secondary thoroughfare famous as a red-light district and a short-cut for motorists through town. Rampant and insensitive commercial development in the middle of the twentieth century has left King Street with a bizarre mixture of huge warehouses clad in corrugated steel standing next to intact fifteenth- and sixteenth-century merchant's houses.

The vast scale of the defunct brewery buildings and the nearby concrete batching plant completely dominate the remaining historic gems that define the original character of the locality. As in the Kirkgate area of Leeds, our approach to this site is to perform a kind of 'dentistry', although in this case the amount of clearance required is greater thus providing bigger areas for redevelopment. The overall aims are threefold:

- To revitalize King Street

- To bring public activity down to the river

- To provide an attractive pedestrian transition zone (via a footbridge) between the eastern side of the river and the city centre

Our design for the area provides a mixed-use development of speciality shops and a restaurant quarter with loft apartments above. These will work with the existing cultural attractions, which include Dragon Hall Museum, the Waterfront Club (music), Wensum Lodge (adult education), and our new building for the Museum of Costume, which celebrates Norwich's famous collection that currently cannot be displayed to the public.

Working around the old buildings and the faint outlines of the historic lanes (some only evident from old maps), we have planned a new quarter

Figure 14.9: St Anne's Wharf, Norwich. Elevation to river.

of blocks, squares, riverside promenades and alleys, which use the naturally sloping topography and concentrate views between King Street and the river.

A new square at the bend in the river is taken as an urban design generator. From this a 'run' of new buildings is to be developed, four to five storeys in height with a module and gable-ended forms that work in rhythm with existing old waterfront warehouses. With plenty of full-height glazing and first-floor terraces for the restaurants, the loft apartments use elevations of horizontal timber boarding used in traditional ways with modern fenestration and roof forms.

Figure 14.10: St Anne's Wharf, Norwich. Elevation to King Street.

Figure 14.11: St Anne's Wharf, Norwich. Perspective view of King Street.

Another important 'run' of new buildings is on King Street itself where the demolition of the massive bulk of the brewery will allow more modest three- and four-storey terraces to be created, emphasizing a module of five metres and bringing roof lines down to achieve a comfortable parity with neighbouring historic structures.

For much of the new development we are utilizing the massive ground slab and piles of the brewery (built in 1971); the remains of a medieval priory lie entombed beneath! The new architecture is of steel, concrete and structural timber with panels of brick, render and boarding to create façades that are not completely alien to the old stalwarts, which have stood nearby for so many centuries. At ground level we are creating an essentially pedestrian environment where cars are subservient and most of the car parks hidden from view. Each elevation is important because it is visible to the public gaze. The urban design strategy is to create sequences of spaces and views to surprise and delight, and yet offer security. The evening economy will be vital to our scheme and consequently the lighting and night atmosphere are receiving special attention to make it an exciting area but safe enough to walk around.

The proposed uses in St Anne's Wharf respond to demand, and a perceived need within Norwich city centre. An enlightened planning department within the City

Council is playing its part by supporting infrastructure improvements that would not be financially viable for the developer to carry out. Architecturally, we have striven to create a bold modern scheme that sits comfortably with its ancient neighbours and does not smother them. If too much reverence to antiquity leads to excessive design restraint, it can be a bad thing.

Conclusion

Whilst working on the projects in Leeds and Norwich, I am very conscious that in fifty years time (or less!) the social and economic life of these quarters might have radically changed. Part of our thinking is always to design with that in mind: to make our buildings, both in structure and plan, robust enough to be adapted for new uses and yet maintain their contribution to what must be a constantly evolving urban pattern.

In the historical development of the fabric of two cities, these are our humble contributions created, we hope, with skill and wisdom on our terms. They may stand the test of time or they may not; perhaps it does not does matter. Cities, by their nature, are forever changing – they must always evolve.

A Continental perspective
The second chamber of the Netherlands parliament, de Tweede Kamer, The Hague

15

Pi de Bruijn de Architekten Cie, Amsterdam

Summary

The Netherlands, like the United Kingdom, has a long history of fine urban planning and a strong sense of history. That history, however, has not stifled a confidence in using the technology of the day nor an ability to look confidently to the future. Pi de Bruijn's description of the process that led to the construction of de Tweede Kamer at The Hague, shows a pragmatic nation at work that is not afraid to open the debate to public scrutiny and explore all avenues until an appropriate solution is found.

By the mid 1970s the Dutch Parliament was fast outgrowing its existing historic buildings and was unable to meet the fundamental demands of democratic government set down in the Netherlands Public Administration Act, which call for transparency and openness of government action. Two options were available: to expand around the existing site, or move to an alternative more spacious location.

Through a four-year process of open competition that was narrowed down to a working group of three selected architects, a realistic solution was agreed. The story is one of collaboration rather than confrontation. It shows a gradual movement towards a solution that respects and uses the existing buildings, whilst adding modern architecture that contrasts and sets off the fabric of the past and achieves the openness and accessibility at the heart of Dutch democracy.

Pi de Bruijn's story shows a refreshing attitude for policy makers and the professions. The final urban infill provides a testimony to the quality that can be achieved through careful research, genuine dialogue, open minds, a will to listen to all interests, but not to compromise. The new parliament buildings at The Hague are a reflection of Dutch response to history. In a country that has a long tradition of high-quality urban design, and a sense of continuity and harmony, they have never been afraid to embrace a 'modern architecture', which is blended with an understanding of context and continuity.

The context of the Netherlands

The typical centres of Dutch cities predominantly have kept their historical grain. This not only applies to major cities such as Amsterdam, The Hague and Utrecht, but equally to medium-sized towns such as Maastricht and Groningen and the vast range of small regional centres such as Delft and Gouda. Dutch urban centres generally are well conserved due to state subsidies, which are granted for urban regeneration or to remodel and rebuild listed buildings.

However, this also means that adding new, large-scale programmes to urban areas in the Netherlands can rarely take place without overcoming major obstacles. There are technical as well as logistical problems to be solved, largely due to the small-scale, granular, character of many central areas, but even more pressing are the inevitable debates that arise when plans for renewal are prevented. The particular projects that elicit highly charged emotional reactions from local residents and other interest groups include high-rise buildings and those designed in contemporary styles of architecture.

In addition to public debate, new buildings in Dutch urban areas require compliance with complex planning and zoning procedures that are complicated by the sheer numbers of interested parties (landowners, proprietors of buildings). Frequently, the assignment is itself granted by various parts of the same local authority, involving a variety of disparate public and private sector parties. Everyone wants a say in these projects, which often take years to complete. Therefore, due to the length of time taken, there is also a very real danger that programmes are changed and expectations and preferences adjusted by the commissioning clients. These restrictions make stringent demands on architects. Patience and perseverance are required both in design and project organization.

Figures 15.1 & 15.2: Aerial views of de Tweede Kamer showing the historical grain of its setting.

Establishing requirements

The new building for the House of Representatives at The Hague has a long prior history. In 1863, Willem III organized an international architectural competition for a new palace to accommodate the Parliament of the Netherlands. Twenty-seven designs were entered but they were found to be poor in quality and too expensive to implement. At the beginning of the twentieth century a new building was once again under discussion as the number of elected representatives had increased from 55 to 100 and more space was required. Six architects, including Berlage and De Bazel, produced designs. The costs, (some 21 million Dutch guilders) once again constituted a stumbling block. The decision was then taken to restore the old chamber along with a number of other rooms.

Between 1945 and 1956, along with developing public and media interest in the workings of the House, the number of representatives increased yet again. A shortage of space meant that there was not only insufficient space for the Representatives but also a lack of space for the public, which directly conflicted with the demands for transparency and openness of government actions of the Netherlands Public Administration Act.

In 1970, under growing pressure for public access, a group of MPs advocated that serious consideration should be given to a new building. An attractive and stylish building was required, complete with a chamber and good accommodation for public tribunes, offices, a hotel, radio and TV studios, a swimming pool, gym and recreation areas with showers, and garage parking for 600 vehicles. Five years later a report was published containing recommendations for such a new building, together with the applicable programme of demands. Pre-judging the need to expand, the Ministry of Housing and Planning (VROM) had already purchased the buildings adjoining the existing house in order to forestall the need to relocate outside The Hague and allow plans to be pursued for the new House on the traditional site of government.

The first competition

A competition was held in 1977 to develop *de Tweede Kamer* with a budget of 150 million Dutch guilders. The participants were asked to provide a design that reflected 'democracy', 'public access to government', and an 'open relationship between the electorate and the elected'. The brief was ill defined, with open questions as

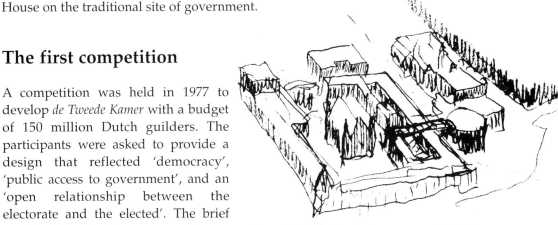

Figure 15.3: De Tweede Kamer conceptual sketch.

to the 'new methods of working and holding meetings' and no clear dimensions for the floor area that was available or required. The outcome was that the jury could not decide on any of the one hundred and eleven entries being of sufficient quality, and the competition was aborted at the end of 1978.

Parliament and the public were losing patience and becoming increasingly irritated. To achieve progress VROM decided to invite tenders for a multiple assignment. Three architects including myself were asked to make a plan. In order to ensure that communications went smoothly between the architects and the Ministry, a management team was appointed to act as a sounding board and facilitator. During the initial meetings between architects and management team, the fact that the programme of demands lacked clarity was addressed. The points that needed clarifying were ideological issues such as public access versus security and the shape and size of the House itself. The total volume of the proposed new building was dealt with yet again as calculations showed that the space requirements of the MPs already exceeded the parameters of the competition by some 15 per cent. Altogether the projects concerned 24,000 square metres of net floor space, not including the garage space of 8,000 square metres. This amounted to three times the area of the current building, which somehow had to fit on the same site with minimum impact on the historical city centre.

Initial proposals

Thinking about the design for the new building was initiated within our design team by investigating the constraints and preconditions of the site. From the outset it was clear that the extensive programme of demands would not readily fit into the parameters of the site and the designated height limits. An initial study was undertaken, which provided a systematic comparison between the necessary and available space (supply and demand). The analytical nature of this study meant that the consequences of the various design choices could be charted and made explicit. Moreover, the users of the building could exercise their influence during the design phase to steer things in a practical direction. On the basis of this study, a thorough analysis was made of the space available. The area covered by the plan, including the sites available for the new building and the existing accommodation, was subjected to both quantitative and qualitative reviews.

The second basic component of the study was the analysis of the programme of demands. A distinction was made between spaces that had an office, meeting room or store room function. These spaces were categorized according to the different preconditions that applied to them. A further distinction was made between the requirements of the MPs and how much of the existing buildings could be deployed. This quantitative approach allowed us to show that, when the requirements of the programme were honoured in their entirety, a new building

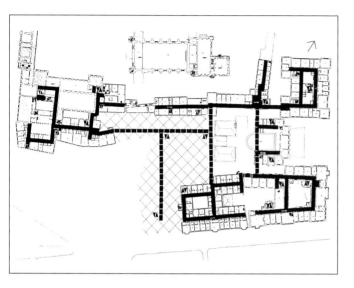

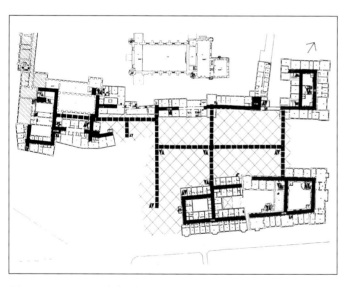

Figure 15.4: Research for the initial proposals included studies of the characteristics of the area.

would be needed with a volume far in excess of the space available on the site. With this data the foundations were laid for a dialogue with the client that thoroughly reviewed the priorities implicit in the programme of demands. Based on the analysis of supply and demand, a series of 40 options were generated, which could be classified into eight basic types. From these, a shortlist of six were proposed for further review. Scale models were constructed, which highlighted the tension between the programme of demands and the spatial conditions.

The final design for the multiple assignment (one of the six models) contained key symbolic elements such as a north-south axis, parallel with the structure of the street plan of The Hague; an east-west axis intersecting this; a shift eastwards of the focal point, which had traditionally been the *Binnenhof*; and a reversal of the leitmotif of the *Ridderzaal*, formerly the House of Representatives, which in the new building was changed from an introverted perspective into one with maximum visibility. The height of the buildings varied from three to thirteen floors (for the office spaces). The main courtyard was retained as a logical space between The Hague woods, the *Malieveld*, the *Plein* and the *Binnenhof*.

Towards a proposal

With the context and objectives agreed, the three architects submitted their plans at the end of 1979, which were exhibited for a number of months so that members of the public could understand, reflect and comment. The Government and the Netherlands Building Department, who were commissioning the project, had in the meantime recognized the unrealistic nature of the programme. The committee that had been charged with making a review of the three plans refrained from making a decision. In its report, the committee concluded that the next stage should consider the limitations of the site as it applied to the programme. The onus was on the Netherlands Building Department, ultimately the client, to reconsider their demands. Tjeerd Dijkstra, the State Architect, advised support for Architekten Cie's proposal with its explicit recognition of the tension between old and new spaces, and its formal more rational architecture. The final decision was to appoint an architect (de Architekten Cie) rather than select a scheme, and to further review and investigate the options for development around the site.

The programme redefined

A detailed prior study conducted in the light of the multiple assignment formed an excellent starting point for the new research phase. The assignment by the Ministry had four parts: to research possibilities of limiting the programme of demands; assess the opportunities of fitting all the necessary components of the programme into a single new building; review the possibility of acquiring buildings in the vicinity of the *Binnenhof*, which could then be subsumed into the plan for the multiple assignment. Models then were developed and a working party formed, which consisted of delegates from the Netherlands Building Department, the construction steering committee for the Houses of Parliament, and the architect.

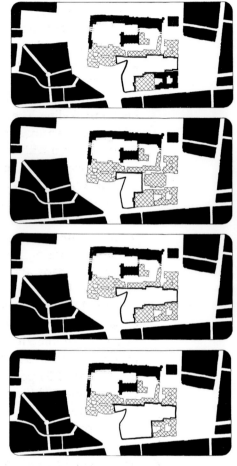

Figure 15.5: Options were assessed comparing the sites and buildings available.

Figure 15.6: The historical skyline of the area was carefully considered.

The research method used was a refined version of the study we had already conducted. The size and location of the new construction volume would be determined by three variables: the urban context, the available space, and the programme of demands. The new assessment resulted in a careful and cautious positioning of the new into the historical *Binnenhof* area, with a sympathetic relationship between new and old building heights that would not disturb the historical skyline. The space available now included three 'new' existing buildings, which had been acquired while the programme of demands remained the same (for the time being) with its 25,600 square metres.

The research was conducted in an iterative manner; we looked and reviewed without knowing any of the answers in advance. After the working party had first concerned itself with the quantitative aspects of the assignment, we then went on to review the qualitative aspects of the programme. In July 1981 we presented the results of our investigations.

The research on floor area demand reduced the requirement by 16 per cent, whilst the space available was increased by the acquisition of two additional buildings. Eight options were assessed and the accommodation programme compared with the sites and buildings available.

Capacity was constrained by well-defined planning demands for the site, which allowed a maximum height of 18 metres and a ratio of building footprint to site area of 50 per cent. Four models fell outside these criteria and the remaining four were subjected to the qualitative criteria of function (space utilization, usability, parking and security) and urban planning (accessibility, image, context, monumentality, and architectural history).

The new building positioned in the central area and along the *Hofstraat* was then put forward as the preferred model. This was the only model that met all the preconditions and remained below the permissible building height of 18 metres. It was adopted by the Netherlands Building Department and the House of Representatives and was recommended for further development. De Architekten Cie were appointed to prepare a definitive design.

Figures 15.7 & 15.8: Conceptual sketches showing height and massing of building.

The definitive design

In urban planning terms, the location of the new building and the adjoining buildings along the east-west axis is well-aligned with the grain of the centre of The

Hague. The complex for *de Tweede Kamer* is at a point where three very different, but vital, city squares are situated (*Binnenhof*, *Plein*, and *Hofplaats*). This makes the location accessible: from the *Binnenhof* there is access reserved for users, and from the other squares access is provided to the public.

The programme for the building falls functionally into three categories: offices, meeting rooms and the main hall or chamber. The offices are situated primarily in existing buildings that have been renovated. The meeting rooms and chamber, with its public amenities, are all situated in the new building. The main characteristic of this design is the development of a new axis, parallel with the *Binnenhof* and the *Ridderzaal*. Spatially, a complementary relationship is established between the new building and the old building with the *Binnenhof*. The new building consists of four parts that are separate elements, which form a total composition: a central atrium, meeting blocks, the new chamber, and the corner building. The central atrium is 24 metres high and 100 metres long and forms a *trait d'union* between the old and new, and constitutes the more important element that gives structure to the new building.

The final design is no longer a new building in the traditional and customary senses of the words. The office spaces are all situated in existing buildings adjoining the construction site and, to a limited extent, can be found in the corner building. The central atrium, at the heart of the new

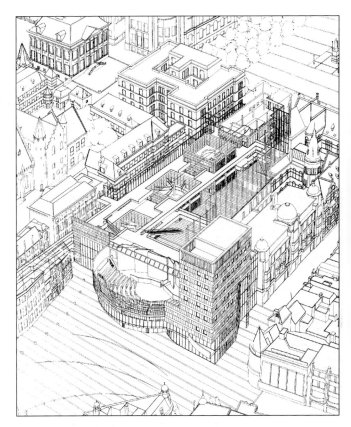

Figure 15.9: Axonometric of the new building and its surroundings.

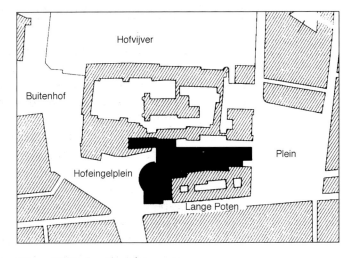

Figure 15.10: Location plan.

House of Representatives, serves as a focus for a colourful and varied set of buildings with different purposes and styles, varying from Functionalist to Dutch Renaissance. In the new building there are only a few blocks of meeting rooms, public areas, traffic provisions, and of course, the Chamber itself. The formal autonomy of the design, so appreciated by Dijkstra, evolved into a structure in which both the new building and the adjacent blocks form a single, integrated whole. The *Binnenhof* complex, which formerly had been fragmented and seen by users as chaotic and unfinished, is now complete and is harmoniously woven into its urban context.

Figure 15.11: View from Hofeingelplein showing the parliament chamber.

Figure 15.12: View across the Plein showing the politicians' glazed lounge.

Conclusion: analysis before design

Reviewing the way that the plans were made for *de Tweede Kamer*, the conclusion to be drawn is that the design developed not purely from a conceptual exercise more from an intense, and as far as possible objective, analytical process. The analysis we had made prior to the design phase ultimately proved to be vital for the rapid progress required of the subsequent research and design phases. Unclear, ambiguous and contradictory programmatic demands proposed by the client were subjected to close scrutiny and the issues broken down into discrete parts to allow decisions to be taken. Intense consultations held during the research phase between the architect, decision makers and all the parties involved, meant that a great deal of mutual respect was created between the different interests so, after the research phase, no real differences of opinion occurred.

More important than rapid progress, which was the prime concern of the House of Representatives, the analytical preparatory work supported the design itself. The analysis opened the possibility to reduce the floor-space requirement, extend the area covered by the plan, retain the buildings on the historical *Lange Poten*, and reappraise the need to demolish the Supreme Court building. The demolition of the Supreme Court had been a concern of a number of the interest groups and, without good arguments, plans that required demolition would be doomed to failure.

The experience we gained with *de Tweede Kamer* shows that a good architect requires analytical skills in order to support unquestioned 'pure' design talents. The architect working on complex projects in an historical context needs insight into the political and social issues that surround a project, coupled with good negotiating skills. Subsequent projects have reinforced this view, both for the area of *Beursplein* in central Rotterdam and for the extension of the *Concertgebouw* in Amsterdam, where careful analysis and a study of options in the initial stages have reaped ample rewards later. Time spent thinking and achieving client understanding and agreement at the beginning reduces construction delays later and assures quality.

Instead of wrestling with architectural concepts at the beginning of a project, I ask myself a very brave question. 'Should something be built here?' New buildings are not always better than reusing existing ones, as amply demonstrated by the new complex for the House of Representatives.

Postscript:
conservation through development

John Worthington

Moving with the times

In his analysis of planners' attitudes to conservation, Les Sparks (*Chapter 5*) describes with great clarity the growth of the conservation movement in the early 1970s as a reaction against professional ideals that had become divorced from community opinions. The period of comprehensive redevelopment during the 1950s and 1960s is typified by an arrogance of professionals, the desire of developers to start afresh, and the distancing of local politicians from their grass-root constituents. The 1969 Skeffington Report on participation in the planning process, reflected a growing dissatisfaction with the public separation from decisions on the environment. The outcome was a proliferation of local conservation groups, amenity societies, and powerful voices from outside the traditional professions. Journalists such as Christopher Booker,[1] and historians such as Marcus Binney and Kenneth Powell (SAVE Britain's Heritage) provided an alternative and popular perspective. The result, often quite unfounded, was a growing divide between the architectural and development professions and the conservationists, who were personified as aiming to freeze the past and stop change. In reality, the two polarities of the conservationists 'retaining and replicating' and the architects starting afresh, were growing closer together.

Conservation, as expressed through world organizations and charters, was developing from showing a concern not merely for monuments but to a wider interest in placemaking.[2] Whilst the early congresses and manifestoes of Madrid (1904) and Athens (1931) focused on the conservation of historic monuments and artifacts, the Athen's Charter of 1933 was showing a concern for context:

'Architectural assets must be protected whether found in isolated buildings or urban aggregations.' By 1981, the Burra Charter for the conservation of places of cultural significance had as its second article the statement that: 'The aim of conservation is to retain or recover the cultural significance of a place and must include the provision for its security and maintenance and its future.' Today, the retention of the spirit of a place and a way of life (the cultural landscape) is given equal importance to the conservation of an artefact. The disciplines of conservation and urban design are colliding, with stimulating results. As our perception of historical associations widens, areas for renewal are increasingly associated with places of historic or cultural value. Changes in industry and the political, economic and social structures have left icons of past glory under-utilized and decaying in areas of economic decline. In addition to the millions of square metres of industrial buildings of historic and architectural significance, can now be added redundant and changing defence, hospital and administrative office building stock.

The speed of social, economic and technological change is placing a great strain on the retention of the quality of historic buildings. York, a world-recognized historic centre, could decay unless it is prepared to continue to change and reinforce its economic well-being and retain its commercial vitality. In the last ten years, with improved technology and rail transport, though the annual visitor number of three million people has remained steady, the profile has changed. Fifteen years ago, with slower trains, the visitor pattern included an overnight stay. Today the journey from Edinburgh to London can be achieved comfortably in a day with a lunch-time break to see the sites of York. A conservation strategy is part of a wider urban and economic renewal strategy. Improved rail connections and telecommuting make York an attractive destination for 'travellers' as well as 'trippers' and a haven for high-quality creative businesses with a global customer base. A sense of place and local character, epitomized in history, is a growing attraction for the discerning business and its knowledge workers.[3]

Regeneration through heritage

The Business in the Community *Regeneration Through Heritage* initiative, with the support of the Prince of Wales, aims to regenerate areas of economic hardship by regenerating the industrial heritage. Saltaire, Bradford's Little Germany, and Dean Clough Mill near Halifax are shining examples of regenerated industrial buildings, but large amounts of redundancy and economic decline in places such as Ancotes in Manchester and Port Clyde near Glasgow still demand attention. Current projects being supported by *Regeneration Through Heritage* include: Wakefield Waterfront, Sowerby Bridge, and the Centennial Mill at Preston. All reflect a strategy that is a balanced approach between building and business renewal (*Figure 1*). The building conservation approach can vary from the light touch of 'do it

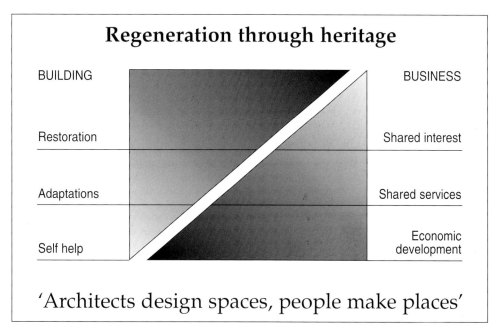

Figure 1: Regeneration through heritage.

yourself' and 'sweat equity' to a comprehensive conservation programme of restoration. The business approach may vary in resources from a comprehensive economic development programme of a development corporation to initiating a community of local businesses with shared interests. There is growing recognition that conservation success will be through a balanced programme of building and community regeneration, renewing both the fabric and the spirit of the place.

Making places

Paradoxically, the opportunities for revitalizing many of our declining historic areas requires both conservation and development: conserving and adapting the old for its cultural and historic value, whilst simultaneously demolishing those parts that reduce effective and flexible use, and building new to provide usable and adaptable space for a wider range of functions. In his Reith lectures[4] Richard Rogers argued for compact and sustainable cities that intensify the use of space and breathe life back into our derelict de-industrialized city sites. He argues against 'slavishly restoring old buildings to their supposed original condition.' Over zealous preservation often reduces flexibility and restricts new uses.

Placemaking is now at the heart of conservation. There is a growing recognition amongst those involved with our past that to achieve a living and sustainable solution it is critical to:

- Understand both the characteristics of the building and the organizations available to use it and make it happen

- Pay equal attention to the process of renewal as to the renovation of the product

- Revive the spirit of the area as well as conserve the quality of the fabric

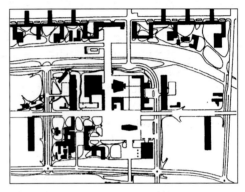

Figure 2: Plans comparing the form of the traditional city (left) – complete, continuous, vibrant – with that of the modern city – fragmented, uniform.

Conservation, as it seeks to retain the continuity of a sense of place, becomes involved with a diversity of interest and expertise to both sustain the fabric and manage the ongoing functions. The successful renewal of an historic area requires teamwork through time, with those interested in the building working in harmony with the place managers.

The principles of urban conservation and urban design perhaps are one. I would define urban design as 'the art of elegantly and meaningfully allocating resources through time, so as to provide a framework to encourage and discipline change.' At the heart of the process is:

- Defining of context and identification of opportunities and constraints

- Setting of achievable and accepted goals through a participative process

- Establishment of a vision for the quality of place

- The agreement of an implementable programme

Conservation management plans have similar objectives. It is ironic that, due to the historic division of professional disciplines, the worlds of urban design and conservation may have been seen in different boxes. Initiatives such as the Urban

Design Alliance,[5] which brings together seven of the professional institutions concerned with improving the quality of urban life, will cross professional boundaries and recognize placemaking as a 'shared responsibility.'

Back to the future

In Continental Europe the sense of integrating the new with the old, to establish a continuity of urban life and a sense of place, has been a continuous tradition. Planners and architects have not lost the confidence of the community in their ability to integrate the new with the old to achieve a vibrant environment. Pi de Bruijn's reorganization of the House of Representatives in the Hague (*Chapter 14*) shows a pragmatic and uninhibited approach to marrying the old with the new. The historic centre of Amsterdam is a continuing story of inserting the new into the old, whether as a Modern Movement façade of the pre-war period, or a careful weaving of new housing into the historic fabric.

Foster and Partners' design for the Cultural Centre at Nîmes (*Chapter 13*) epitomizes the confident and unhibited approach to development in Continental Europe where there has been an unconstrained attitude to architecture throughout the century. This, and other examples in the book, show that there has been a resurgence of this approach by architects in the United Kingdom backed by the confidence of their clients. The Royal Academy and the British Museum, bastions of the establishment in Britain, have taken a leading role in commissioning bold new architecture in recent extensions to their galleries. In Leeds and Norwich John Lyall is regenerating rundown areas by inserting vibrant new buildings into the historic fabric. Meanwhile, Edward Cullinan and Richard MacCormac have built their reputations on designing new buildings for historic areas and their respective designs for modern buildings are timeless in their settings.

The separation between conservationist and architect is blurring. In schools of architecture the missionary zeal of the Modern Movement has mellowed. A respect for the past and an understanding of the 'timeless ways of building' are more accepted as part of every architect's understanding. Conservation is becoming part of the mainstream, and the past is becoming part of the future.

Notes and references

1. BOOKER, Christopher, *The Seventies: portrait of a decade*, Harmondsworth, Penguin, 1980.
2. BAUMANN, Nicholas, *Townscape in Urban Conservation. The impact of the theory of townscape on conservation planning*. IoAAS, The University of York, DPhil. Dissertation, 1996.
3. WORTHINGTON, John, *Reinventing the Work-place*, Oxford, Butterworth, Heinemann, 1997.
4. ROGERS, Richard, *Cities for a Small Planet*, Faber and Faber, 1997.
5. Urban Design Alliance (UDAL) is a group of leading professional bodies launched at a meeting at the Royal Institution of Chartered Surveyors, London, December 1997.

Index